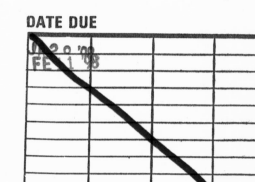

GILDA BERGER

VIOLENCE

AND SPORTS

Franklin Watts ■ *New York* ■ *London* ■ *Toronto* ■ *Sydney* ■ *1990*

Library of Congress Cataloging-in-Publication Data

Berger, Gilda.
Violence and sports / Gilda Berger.
p.   cm.
Includes bibliographical references (p.   ).
Summary: An examination of the causes and effects of the violence
that occurs in sports both among athletes and Fans.
ISBN 0-531-10907-0
1. Violence in sports—Juvenile literature.   [1. Violence in
sports.]   I. Title.
GV706.7.B47   1990
796—dc20   89-28069   CIP   AC

CONTENTS

VIOLENCE AND SPORTS

CHAPTER

INTRODUCTION

- *"If you don't have guts, and you can't take it, you don't belong in hockey," says hockey star Ted Lindsay.*[1]

- *"I had a license to kill for 60 minutes a week. My opponents were all fair game and when I got off the field, I had no regrets. It was like going totally insane," says football star Alex Karras.*[2]

- *"It's a great test of character if a man can play hurt. It shows what kind of competitor he is. A good, hard-nosed competitor does it," says basketball coach Bill Sharman.*[3]

- *"Getting hit is scary. The last thing you remember is collapsing over the plate, and the next thing you remember is riding in the ambulance," says baseball star Roger Maris.*[4]

- *"I have to change [before entering the ring]. I have to leave the goodness out and bring all the bad in, like Dr. Jekyll and Mr. Hyde," says heavyweight boxing champion Larry Holmes.*[5]

- *"The contract is either you hurt the opponent or he hurts you," says psychiatrist Dr. Charles M. Pierce.*[6]

Sports violence is a worldwide phenomenon that seems to be growing more and more serious. In Canada, a government investigation of hockey violence concludes that a "sick situation" exists at all levels of the country's favorite sport. In England, it was recently revealed that one in four male spectators have taken part in soccer hooliganism, which is believed to have resulted in at least three murders. In Italy, a rugby player came off the field bleeding and in pain because someone bit off part of his left ear. Several players and officials have been stomped to death by angry fans on soccer fields in Latin America. And in the United States, successive World Series have ended in fan riots.[7]

What is sports violence? And why have brawling, beating, and even killing become part of the games people play?

THE PROBLEM

It is often difficult to identify violence in sports. The distinction between senseless viciousness and the normal rough-and-tumble of play is often hard to make. But, generally speaking, sports violence is defined as any act by a player, coach, or fan that has as its *primary* goal inflicting pain or causing injury. This excludes injuries that are *incidental* to the normal way the game is played.

A player hitting an opponent with a clenched fist, driving a helmet into someone's body, poking an elbow into another's eye, or slamming a hockey stick across a rival's back—all are examples of violence in sports. A fan tossing a can of beer at a player, walloping a rival fan, or rioting in the streets after a game also constitutes sports violence.

Some experts point out that violence in sports is almost exclusively a male behavior. They associate it with *machismo*, the exaggerated sense of masculine pride. Defeat is seen as a severe blow to *machismo*, and resorting to violence in athletic contests is thought to be a way of protecting one's pride and manhood.

Many athletes have a double standard as regards morality in sports and in everyday life. As one high school basketball player put it, "In life . . . there are so many people to think about. . . . In sports you're free to think about yourself."[8] This self-centeredness is considered necessary in athletes who are playing to win.

While competing, some athletes tend to think of the opposing team members as not merely opponents who are human beings just like themselves but as enemies. This reduces their sense of responsibility; it releases them from the usual demands of morality. Hurting the "enemy" to get him out of the game or using intimidation to interfere with his performance becomes acceptable behavior. In any other area of life, those same athletes would consider such acts as immoral. But in sports, they feel, anything goes—as long as it helps to win the game or to come in first in the race.

Many argue that sports have always been violent and that today things are no better or worse than years ago. But the evidence contradicts this.

Estimates of injuries and deaths among participants in the various sports can be used as one measure of the violence. No one list is complete, and the numbers vary greatly from source to source. But, according to the figures of the National Safety Council and some others, each year sports participants sustain about 20 million injuries serious enough to require medical attention. Of these, about 6 million injuries leave long-lasting damage ranging from scars to paralysis or death.[9]

Quite often, sports violence extends far beyond the playing field. University athletes are more likely than other students to be accused of rape, assault, break-ins, and drug trafficking. In fact, a 1986 survey of 350 colleges found that athletes had been involved in at least 61 sexual assaults between 1983 and 1985. Football and basketball players were 38 percent more likely to be implicated in such crimes than the average male college student.[10] Furthermore, there are indications that the rate of violence by athletes off the playing field is also on the rise.

The reasons for the upsurge in violence among college athletes are wide and diverse. Some say that college coaches recruit players who can help them win games, regardless of their personal or academic qualifications. To take one example: Roosevelt Potts signed an agreement on February 8, 1989, to play with the team at Northeast Louisiana University. Yet, just two months earlier, he had pleaded guilty to aggravated battery for firing a shotgun at a crowd outside a barroom.[11]

Coaches frequently recruit youngsters from disparate, often disadvantaged, backgrounds. In college, these young people are exposed to experiences, expectations, and demands that they may have difficulty handling. Severe culture shock sometimes results in violence.

Some coaches have been blamed for "coddling" the athletes and excusing their crimes. For example, Lefty Driesell, former basketball coach at Maryland, called a woman three times to try to persuade her not to press charges of sexual misconduct against one of his players, Herman Veal.[12] Melvin C. Ray, assistant professor of sociology at Mississippi State University, says, "Athletes are put on a pedestal. They are given almost free rein to do what they want as long as their teams are in the Top 20."[13]

The same potential for violence and aggressiveness can be seen in professional sports. For the "pros," the style of play has become "progressively dirtier."[14] Players are not above using "cheap shots"—the poke with the elbow, the kick in the shins—to win games. Their opponents then retaliate, and the violence escalates. "It's much more violent than people know," football player Tom Mack said a few years back, "slugging, punching, people really trying to intimidate. There are not many fights, but a lot of intimidatory tactics, and most intimidation is violent."[15] Such intimidation and cheap shots, some say, are the backbone of professional sports.

Recently, the Philadelphia Flyers were playing a final match against the Montreal Canadiens. Suddenly, faced with defeat, the Flyers resorted to the type of hockey for which they have become notorious. They stopped playing and started punching.

When asked to explain their behavior, the Philadelphia players gave a number of reasons. The first was frustration at having their offense killed by the Canadiens. The second was anger at an unpenalized check by a Canadien on a Flyer in an earlier game. And when one of the Flyers threw a particularly hard, bone-crushing check at that particular Canadien, the Flyers management backed him up. "We don't like the incident," said the Flyers general manager, Bobby Clarke, "but we like the fact that he was sticking up for his teammate."[16]

COMPULSION TO WIN

The need to win in sports begins very early. The Little Leaguer or young hockey player, wherever he or she lives, gets the same message: Be number one. Win at all costs Unless you are a winner you'll never be truly happy or satisfied with yourself.

The CBS television program *60 Minutes* focused on the Pop Warner children's football league in Hollywood, Florida. Coaches were shown insulting kids who made mistakes and urging players to play rough to win.[17]

In general, young players are encouraged to imitate the toughest, most argumentative players, not necessarily the most skilled. A constant stream of sloganeering and drilling to win starts at age eight or so. By the time they get to high school and beyond, players have learned the lessons of violent and dangerous behavior, of hostility and aggressiveness, and of rule breaking when they can get away with it.

Most people accept the idea that instilling a competitive spirit in children helps build character. But some feel that competitive sports have the opposite effect. After a steady diet of messages to win, the youngsters who fail in sports can suffer a loss in self-esteem. Studies show that they may then feel a need to compensate by becoming overly aggressive, even in non-sport situations.

Athletic success is so important to a boy's peer group status that being labeled a loser either by oneself or by others may encourage antisocial behavior. One high school has a "Hall of Shame" list of the names of boys who quit football. The result of being on the list is that the boy is shunned by his classmates.[18] By being thrust into an environment that is relatively vicious before he or she can handle the strain, an athlete can, at the very least, be robbed of the thrill of competing, which exists apart from the thrill of winning.

The pressure to win at all costs is especially intense on the college and professional levels. If a team has a losing season, the coach is often fired. Athletes are encouraged to play while injured, sometimes by coaches whose jobs are on the line, sometimes for the good of the team, and sometimes because it is considered the "manly" thing to do. Athletes have incurred many permanent injuries as a result of playing while hurt.

This need to win was most clearly expressed by footballer Vince Lombardi when he said, "Winning isn't everything. It's the only thing." And, "To play this game you must have a fire in you, and there is nothing that stokes fire like hate."[19]

The drive to compete has been said to be part and parcel of the American fabric of life. Our early ancestors were aggressive and competitive. History records how the first settlers conquered a new land and overcame the resistance of the native Americans. The colonists defied the power of English rule and brought Africans here to be slaves. Later Americans settled the West. They triumphed over hardships and adversity, fought against their fellow countrymen, and engaged in various struggles with foreign powers throughout the world. The striving for gain and advantage appears to have increased hostility and aggressiveness in all Americans. "We can no longer regard hatred and violence as accidents and aberrations," says noted American historian Arthur Schlesinger.[20]

In a society preoccupied with competition and winning, average people need something to latch onto that makes them feel worthwhile, too. Competing can provide that boost. Competitors can feel that by working hard and doing their best, they will win. But the more successful they become, the more intense the pressure becomes. Each athlete must then deal with the strain to keep winning and with the demands to maintain the level of skill that brought him or her to the top in the first place.

Part of the winning ethic of coaches and athletes seems to be one of playing while injured. To play in pain offers proof of courage and team loyalty. It is part and parcel of the spirit of trying to win. Just as inflicting injury is part of the game, so the ability to play while injured gives evidence of one's "manliness."

For many reasons, winners are perceived as heroes— sexually superior, better-looking, and more appealing than others. This so-called halo effect often protects athletes from official reprimands and attaches attributes to them that they may not necessarily possess. Hence, winners are often perceived as being nice guys, sincere and considerate. As basketball great Bill Russell once said, "This business about an athlete being so great is a fiction . . . written by nonathletes who may be acting out their own fantasies."[21]

But even being on top has its problems. After much adulation, money, and pampering, it is not unusual for greed and narcissism to set in. When "top" players lose, they may suffer bitterly. Suddenly, they have no status at all. Winning is essential to feeling good about oneself and therefore justifies doing whatever is necessary to come out first or on top.

No matter how successful the athletes are, the dreams, ambitions, drives, and expectations of financial reward that they hold often clash with reality. People who want to become winners at all costs—or just keep on winning—sometimes resort to the use of drugs in a fruitless attempt to help them meet their goals. The use of drugs to "get up" for a game or to become a better athlete stems as much from society's pressure to win as it does from the influence of our own drug culture.

The athletes who use drugs think at first that the drugs are making them stronger and more combative—and therefore better competitors. Actually, of course, the drug high begins to chip away at their physical condition, and they start to lose the ability to play well and succeed in the sport.

Athletes probably account for about 10 percent of all users of the group of drugs known as steroids.[22] They take steroids because they believe that the drugs increase muscle growth, and they think that the added muscle size will give them more strength, stamina, and speed in competition. Use of the drugs is banned because it gives some athletes an unfair advantage and subjects them to a rather considerable health risk. But, despite doctors' warnings that such use might cause cancer, heart disease, and other health problems, some athletes are willing to risk all for the rewards that come with success in sports.

Just as athletes turn to drugs in their drive to succeed, so they look on violence and aggression as important qualities to cultivate. Thus, the frustrations of losing can lead to on-the-field brawls, locker-room fights, bickering, backbiting, and disloyalty to the team. All too often, the coaches and managers encourage this behavior by considering squabbles and fighting valuable ingredients in building a team's character.

Fighting is also considered the best way to play a winning game and please the crowd at the same time. On-the-field melees and fights are thought to unify the team and raise their spirits. A good, healthy free-for-all goes along with the end-justifies-the-means philosophy put forth by some coaches. After his players brawled with the St. Louis Cardinals during the 1973 season, coach George Allen of the Washington Redskins said that he "loved the fight. . . . If we didn't go out there and fight I'd be worried." He told how he had once encouraged a fracas "just to get 'em going. Just to get 'em all together. . . . Because unless you get 'em all together, unless you have that, you aren't going to be a winner. It's all part of winning."[23]

In hockey, a willingness to slug it out if provoked is encouraged. "Show that you're a winner and can't be pushed around," players tell each other. Those who don't play according to such rules are labeled "wimps."

Insiders argue that athletes don't really mean what they say or do on the field. They are just playing to the crowd and talking for the effect it will have on others. If that is so, others say, they should be honest. Young viewers, especially, at the games or watching on television believe what their heroes do and say. They model their own behavior on that of the professionals. And, of course, player violence leads fans to contribute their own form of violence.

Nowhere can the exhilarating power of the winning obsession be seen and heard more clearly than in spectator violence at the stadium. It is almost as though the crowds that come to watch sports are inspired by and imitate the violent players and coaches that they see before them.

Hometown fans can become frighteningly destructive

when their team is losing. They sometimes even target the very players they had come to cheer on. At times, the fans turn their frustration against the losing coach. When onetime Green Bay Packer coach Dan Devine had a string of game losses, he and his family were harassed, spat on, and insulted. Eventually, his dog was shot dead.[24]

Psychology professor Delia S. Saenz of the University of Notre Dame has tried to explain this loss of control, especially at baseball, football, and basketball games. She believes it starts with arousal to a state that leads people to do what they wouldn't do under normal circumstances. They no longer think as individuals. No one feels personally responsible as long as he or she is doing what everyone else is doing. So, she says, "the crowd moves itself along."[25]

Former baseball commissioner A. Bartlett Giamatti saw it somewhat differently. He said that the fan today is a product of our new society. This fan has his own ideas of behavior. Typically white, male, and eighteen to thirty years old, he "uses the rock concert as his model of behavior—that is, he goes to a stadium to drink and meet people; the game is secondary."[26]

REDUCING VIOLENCE IN SPORTS

Some people think we should not be alarmed by aggression and violence in sports. They believe that sports serve as a positive outlet, or catharsis, for the aggressive drive we all have. Competition eases the tensions and stresses of modern life, they say. The identification fans develop with players, teams, or events allows them to get the same benefits from the action as the athletes. Competition channels the aggressive drive. Without competitive sports, they insist, we would have an even more violent society.

Those who disagree hold that aggression in sports increases the competitiveness and violence in our society.

They believe that sports teach players that aggression is acceptable behavior for getting back at someone, helping to win, and seeing that justice is done. "Beat 'em," "be tough," "fight," and "kill him" suggest that violence is permitted and necessary. Violent acts lead to further aggression and a lowering of inhibitions. In short, they say, competitive sports contribute to the violent society we have today.

Many who would like to eliminate violence in sports have put forth recommendations for reducing aggression on the sports field. Most ideas focus on setting up tighter rules and penalties against fighting and other forms of violence for the players. But reducing the violence that now surrounds so many athletic contests may require more than this. Coaches may have to do more to lower the levels of aggression among their players by creating a good postgame atmosphere. Negative comments, especially after a losing game, can fuel already heightened aggressive feelings.

Among the additional ideas that have been suggested are placing limits or completely banning the sale of beer at sporting events, establishing strict rules for fan behavior, and increasing the security force to make sure that the rules are enforced. Even staging the games in empty stadiums and telecasting them from there is a possibility.

Experts say that the uproars off and on the field are caused by a decline in respect for authority throughout professional sports. Also, the escalation in violence may have to do with the longer seasons and the bigger money in sports today compared with twenty to thirty years ago. The longer season tends to result in more frayed nerves and quick tempers. And the higher salaries for players and bigger potential profits for team owners have raised the stakes considerably. The increased pressure makes players snappy, and angry words or gestures are more likely to erupt into blows and violence. If season length and financial concerns are indeed the problem, stiffer penalties and a shorter season may well be the way to bring about changes in behavior.

It is important, however, to differentiate between the truly dangerous violence that takes place on the field and the angry words and dramatic temper tantrums that seem to be put on for the benefit of the fans. Perhaps more sportsmanlike behavior, such as shaking hands or helping someone get up after a fall, might make the point that sports is a game, not a life and death struggle. Without good sportsmanship, as James F. Clarity wrote in the *New York Times*, "Professional sports is a metaphor for winning and losing in life, a show of controlled violence and virtuosity producing fear and joy."[27]

Leo Durocher, former manager of the Brooklyn Dodgers, once told of how he ran out of the dugout to scream at the umpire for what he thought was a bad call. The umpire stopped him in his tracks, though, by saying, "I blew it, Leo, sorry." Durocher then asked for the umpire's permission to stomp around and kick sand for a while. And Durocher did just that until he felt better.

This story is a far cry from the recent trouble Pete Rose, the former Cincinnati Reds manager, had with umpire Dave Pallone. What started as a yelling and finger-waving argument ended with Rose shoving Pallone and being thrown out of the game and slapped with a thirty-day suspension. Because of the need on both sides to appear tough, what started out as a small issue escalated into unnecessary aggression.

Years after Vince Lombardi made his famous statement about the importance of winning, the famous football coach said he had been misquoted. What he had actually said, he claimed, was, "Winning is not everything—but making the effort to win is."[28] San Francisco quarterback John Brodie put it a bit more bluntly: "Sports should be more than winning at any cost, more than beating people up and making money and getting ahead over somebody else's dead body."[29]

Sports do and perhaps should play a vital role in the lives of each of us. They are very important to the spirit of our nation. But their importance should not be greater than our concern about what really matters—preserving the human spirit that connects us to the world and to ourselves. It is time for a message to go out that violence in sports is not acceptable in our society.

CHAPTER

AUTO RACING

■ *In the 1979 Daytona 500 stock car race, three-time champion Cale Yarborough accused competing drivers Donnie and Bobby Allison of forcing him off the track a half mile from the finish. What started as an accusation ended up as a punching, kicking brawl between Yarborough and Donnie Allison that was seen by millions on national TV. The two racing drivers were put on probation. Just a few weeks later they clashed again. While taking part in another race their cars collided, sending three drivers to the hospital.*[1]

■ *Jack Ingram was battling for the lead in the 1986 North Carolina stock car championship race in Asheville when he tangled with two other cars and was forced off the track. To get even, he turned around and drove straight into one of the other cars, injuring driver Ronnie Pressley so badly that he had to be hospitalized.*[2]

■ *Top racing driver Dan Gurney's car caromed off the road in a recent Dutch Grand Prix. In an act of accidental violence, the car completely chopped up a spectator before coming to a stop upside down. Gurney was lucky to get out of it with only a fractured arm and a few broken ribs.*[3]

■ *In the 1981 Indianapolis 500 race, in lap 33 Don Whittington hit the wall, in lap 58 Rick Mears's car caught fire and he and six crewmen were badly burned, and in lap 64 Danny Ongais hit the wall and suffered a fractured leg and internal injuries.*[4]

The message is clear: auto racing, or motor racing, as it is also called, is probably the most violent, dangerous, and deadly of all competitive sports. Tiny but enormously powerful cars spin and hit walls, burn, and come apart. People get hurt, and some die. As Stirling Moss, one of auto racing's all-time greats, put it, "Racing is a kind of Russian roulette. You never know when the chamber will come up loaded."[5]

The figures from the annual Indy 500 race alone tell us much about the violence in racing. At the very first race, in 1909, one driver, two mechanics, and two spectators were killed.[6] Of the 492 drivers who raced in the Indy 500 through 1987, 130—or over 26 percent—have died in racing accidents. Of the thirty-five winners of the race who have died, fourteen—or 40 percent—were killed on auto racing tracks![7]

HISTORY AND BACKGROUND

Racing dates all the way back to the times of the ancient Greeks and Romans. The only difference between then and now is that the drivers in times long past used chariots, two-wheeled carts pulled by horses, instead of superpowerful automobiles.

In those olden times, about forty chariots entered each race. All of them would run the length of the track, circle a column, and return to the starting point. Any number of bloody, fatal accidents occurred along the course. But the start of the race, when all the drivers would jostle for good positions, and the turns, when men, horses, and chariots would pile up in a huge, writhing mass, were the worst moments of the event.

Also, as the chariots entered the final straightaway, the horses were sometimes purposely frightened by race officials. Often, they would rear up (rise on their back legs), overthrow the chariot, and then bolt the remaining length of the race at breakneck speed. Since traditionally the reins were tied around the driver's waist, this usually meant that the athlete was dragged along the ground for the final stretch.[8]

Automobile racing probably began in France in 1894. Just four years later, the first racing driver was killed. And only nine years after that, the full extent of the danger of auto racing truly became apparent. At least five drivers and twelve pedestrians lost their lives in the 1903 Paris to Madrid road race.[9]

In some sports, the amateurs and beginners sustain the most injuries; the professionals and experienced participants are usually able to avoid danger. Not so in auto racing. The stars, the veteran drivers, and the first-timers are equally prone to injuries—or even death—without discrimination.

Just before the 1961 Italian Grand Prix, the outstanding driver, Wolfgang von Trips, said, "The line between maximum speed and crashing is so thin, so thin. It could happen tomorrow." For von Trips, crashing didn't come the next day; it came just a few hours after he made that statement. His car spun out of control at 150 miles an hour and ripped into a crowd of spectators, leaving him and fifteen onlookers dead. He had indeed crossed the thin line.[10]

A DO-OR-DIE ATTITUDE

The secret of success in auto racing—whether it be that of a stock car or a top-of-the-line Formula I—is to push the car to its absolute maximum speed on straightaways as well as on turns and curves but never to exceed that maximum. Some drivers try for an edge. They try to take a turn just a tiny bit faster than they should. If they are lucky, they make it and win the race; if they are unfortunate, they fail to win the race—and perhaps even lose their lives.

Ricardo Rodriguez of Mexico is often cited as an example—or perhaps victim—of just such a do-or-die attitude. By the time Rodriguez was fifteen years of age, he was already racing. At nineteen he became the youngest driver ever to enter the top ranks of auto driving, the Grand Prix circuit. But at age twenty he took a curve just a little bit too fast and crashed. As the men worked frantically to free him from the wreckage, Rodriguez pleaded with them to save his life. But despite their best efforts and those of his doctors, Rodriguez died of his injuries just a few days later.[11]

With so much death, injury, and mayhem on the track and in the stands, why does auto racing continue to be such a popular sport? Why do over 50 million people a year pay to see motor races of all sorts?

It is generally believed that racing fans are drawn to the track by the specter of injury and destruction. If you ask fans why they attend auto races, many will tell you it is because they admire the skill and daring of the drivers. But others, especially young people, confess that they come because they are intrigued by the prospect of witnessing spectacular accidents and blowups.

Very few observers actually want to witness anyone getting hurt. The ideal race, to their way of thinking, includes a spectacular flip-over accident or collision involving several cars—from which all the drivers walk away.

Yet this craving to experience violence vicariously is so strong that some fans seem almost disappointed when a star driver retires in comparatively good health—instead of driving until an injury or death puts an end to his or her career! When the Argentine superstar driver Julio Fangio left the sport while still quite healthy, he was heavily criticized. A reporter asked him why, and Fangio answered, "My only fault is being alive."[12]

Few drivers, even the most careful, succeed in escaping the danger and violence of auto racing entirely. Take the case of Harry Schell. While most drivers last a couple of years before retiring or being forced to retire because of injuries, Schell was active for a full eleven seasons. During all those years he never came in first in a major race, but he racked up enough seconds, thirds, and fourths to earn a comfortable living. He once commented, "With me racing is a business. I don't take chances."[13] Despite his careful, conservative driving style, though, Schell was killed in an accident in 1970.

As a matter of fact, almost every top racer has had at least one bad accident. Stirling Moss is a good example. Moss was one of the all-time great Grand Prix drivers. He won a total of 466 races, including sixteen Grand Prix meets. His first serious mishap came in Belgium in 1960 when a wheel came off his car as he was speeding along at 140 miles an hour. Moss was thrown out of the car and quite badly hurt, with fractures in both legs, his nose, ribs, and three spinal vertebrae.

Two years later, tragedy struck. Moss was in a race in England and going relatively slowly, only about 100 miles an hour. Because of a long pit stop he was behind many of the other cars and was struggling to move up to the front again. Somehow, he lost control of the car, which flew across the track and a nearby field, smashed into an earthen embankment, and folded in two. It took the track workers a half hour to cut Moss free of the wreckage. In the hospital, he lay in a coma for thirty-eight days. His broken bones included toes, ankles, leg, elbow, shoulder, and cheek. Forty stitches were required to repair his facial injuries alone. The terrible accident left him permanently brain-injured and vision-impaired.[14]

Richie Ginther may hold the record for surviving the worst string of accidents of any driver. In March 1962, Ginther was seriously burned when a new race car he was testing caught fire. Soon after his release from the hospital, Ginther was racing in Holland when another car butted him off the track, causing a number of minor injuries.

Only a few months after that, in a race in Monaco, Ginther's throttle jammed, propelling him forward and preventing him from stopping the car. Without control, he slammed into several other cars on the track. The smashup also knocked a wheel off his car, which flew out and killed one of the spectators.[15]

RACING-RELATED RISKS AND ACCIDENTS

Even when the drivers are not involved in a crash or collision, they may be the victims of violence during the course of a race. Studies show that the driver's heartbeat can be as fast as 200 beats per minute, which is about the speed of a sprinter's heart in a 100-yard dash. The difference is that the sprinter does it for a few minutes at most; the race car driver keeps it up for perhaps three hours in a Grand Prix race![16]

Formula racing cars conform to prescribed specifications as to size, weight, and engine displacement. They usually have a long, narrow body, open wheels, a single-seat open cockpit, and the engine in the rear. The cockpits of the famous Formula I race cars are so tiny and have so little insulation that the temperature can get as high as 160°F. Alain Prost, a leading Grand Prix racer, loses as much as 9 pounds in a race.[17]

Race cars have no suspension systems; every bump in the road sends the metal of the chassis slamming against the bottom of the driver's spine. During a race, professional drivers will shift gears every few seconds. And each change of gears jars the head either forward or backward.

Some drivers have said that every downshift is like getting a punch in the small of the back. Along with this, there is the deafening roar of the engine and the squeal of the tires. And to top it off, there are the powerful centrifugal or centripetal forces on every turn or curve pulling the driver one way or the other.

The most remarkable fact about auto racing is not the number of drivers who get maimed or killed. It is the number who survive the crashes and accidents. One of the most common racing accidents is the spin, an everyday occurrence in auto racing that usually happens when the driver is going too fast into a turn or sharp curve.

There is probably not one driver—dead or alive—who has not spun out a number of times. Most often, though, no one is hurt when a car spins. One reason is that all drivers slow down at curves and therefore approach the spin at a somewhat reduced speed. Also, good drivers have sufficient skills and quick reactions to get out of the spin quickly and easily and are able to continue the race. The single biggest danger of a spin is being hit by nearby drivers.

Another common racing-related accident is shunting. This is the name for two cars touching or scraping each other but not actually colliding. It can happen front to back or side to side. Shunting scratches the paint off the car and dents or rips the sheet-metal body but usually doesn't cause any injuries and doesn't stop the cars from finishing the race.

Flipping over always frightens the spectators but only occasionally harms the drivers. The cars are built to remain rigid, even when resting on the roof. And since the drivers wear helmets and are belted in, they usually only suffer minor injuries at most.

Auto racing accidents, no matter how they happen, can be serious or even deadly. But driver Buddy Baker's accident at the Smokey Mountain roadway in 1968 is truly a funny story that we can enjoy, especially since no one got fatally injured.

During this particular race, Baker, an experienced and competent driver, blew a tire, lost control, and smashed into a concrete wall. He suffered a concussion and some fractured ribs and, of course, had to be taken to the hospital.

The medics drove onto the track and strapped Baker to a stretcher. They slid the stretcher into the back of the old hearse that the track owners used as an ambulance. However, they failed to close the back door securely. As the ambulance driver gunned the engine and took off at full speed, the door flung open, and the stretcher with Baker on top slid out and onto the track—right into the path of the drivers who were still in the race! As Baker later said, "I told myself, 'Ain't this something. Here I survive a crash head on into a cement wall and now I'm gonna get killed on a rolling stretcher.' "[18]

Happily, the other drivers saw the stretcher bouncing across the track and were able to swerve to the side. The ambulance driver finally caught up with Baker and wheeled him back to the hearse. But this time, Baker refused to stay on the stretcher. He insisted on sitting up front with the driver.

Baker's troubles were not over yet, though. While heading to the hospital at top speed, the ambulance driver went through a red light. Suddenly, another car pulled out in front of the hearse/ambulance, forcing the driver to avoid a collision by turning as sharply as he could. As a result, he skidded up onto the sidewalk and into a cluster of garbage cans! The rest of the ride to the hospital continued with one flat tire and no brakes.

Baker was treated at the hospital and released. Although the hearse was waiting there to take him back to the track, Baker refused the offer for obvious reasons and found another ride.

Every year an estimated fourteen or fifteen people are killed in auto races.[19] The number includes drivers, mechanics, and spectators. And the rate of injuries grows. Ten spectator deaths occurred in 1987 alone. In one, a driver lost his wheel at the third turn. The wheel was hit by another car and bounced into the stands, hitting and instantly killing Lyle Kurtenbach, a forty-one-year-old salesman from Rothschild, Wisconsin.[20]

Critics say that the evidence is clearly against auto racing and that the sport should be banned. But supporters of the sport insist that racing is among the most exciting sports of all time. The drivers are adults who are well aware of the risks. And despite the serious nature of the injuries, the rate is still low when compared to other sports. Yet even the most enthusiastic fans agree that more efforts should be made to increase the safety of the sport.

Actually, race driver safety has improved in recent years to some extent. In the last sixteen years, only one driver has been killed on the Indianapolis Speedway compared with thirty-six in the years before 1973. Better materials, plus the fairly new practice of building cars so that they come apart on impact, are credited with the improvement. The quick breakup of the car scatters the energy of the crash and lessens the risk of injury to the driver.

Not long ago, the National Association of Stock Car Auto Racers (NASCAR) instituted some new rules designed to slow down cars and make racing safer. The rules restricted the flow of air and gas to the engine, cutting power by about 200 horsepower. Generally speaking, drivers oppose any regulations that take any excitement from the game. Recently, some criticized the ruling, saying it makes driving even more dangerous. Without power, "You don't have the ability to get out of trouble," says one driver.[21]

In March 1987, the Fédération Internationale du Sport Auto (FISA), which sets international standards for racing cars, decreed that turbo engines be outlawed. Top racers are conforming to these new rules in a grudging way. But presumably, they are continuing their own search to increase safety while keeping the thrills of the sport.

CHAPTER

BASKETBALL

- *"The contact comes with forcing an arm in somebody's ribs, placing an elbow in the small of the back. It's done very subtly, but it's as crisp and hard as you can make it," says Phil Jackson, former Knicks player.*[1]

- *"There are violent blows struck out there. It's a very physical game; contact is a big part of it. . . . . You have to be willing to defend your territory," says Senator Bill Bradley, former star basketball player on the New York Knicks.*[2]

- *"The game has become more physical, there's no question about it," says Jim Boeheim, basketball coach at Syracuse University.*[3]

- *"So much stress is laid today on the winning of games that practically all else is lost sight of," said Dr. James Naismith in 1914, twenty-three years after he invented the game of basketball.*[4]

- *"It just doesn't seem that there were as many fights twenty years ago. Why? The pot at the end of the rainbow is bigger. If you're good, you get a chance to be looked at to get a pro con-tract," says Art Hyland, supervisor of officials, Big East Con-ference.*[5]

The violence on the basketball courts has become so typical that some critics declare that it is getting out of control. The National Basketball Association (NBA) has tried to deal with the violence, but they face many difficulties.

Professional players today are far larger than they were in the early days of basketball. Bigger and bigger bodies flying around a relatively small playing area now results in extreme physicality—sometimes of a violent nature. Increasing the size of the court or raising the height of the baskets might help. But there is little support for such changes. So it is up to everyone—league officials, referees, managers, coaches, players, and fans—to work to keep the violence from growing worse.

HISTORY AND BACKGROUND

Most of the modern sports gradually evolved from ancient games over many centuries. But basketball was the deliberate invention of one American clergyman, Dr. James A. Naismith, in 1891. Dr. Naismith was enrolled at the YMCA Training School in Springfield, Massachusetts, in 1890 and the following year was invited to stay on as an instructor. It was there that he hit on the game of basketball.

Dr. Luther Gulick, head of the athletic department at Springfield, felt that it would help the youth of the country to have an exciting and interesting game that could be played indoors, particularly during the winter months between the football and baseball seasons. He asked his staff to make some suggestions.

Dr. Naismith took up the challenge. The first thing he did was to define some characteristics that he considered desirable in the new sport:

- Stress team pla , not individual performance.
- Easy to learn.
- Playable by eitl r men or women, boys or girls.
- Emphasize spe and skill, not strength, weight, or size.
- Use a ball but bat, glove, or other equipment.
- Play with a ba o large that it can't be hidden.
- Avoid physic ntact.[6]

Finally, Dr. Naisi had the idea of hanging two peach baskets from eith d of the balcony in the YMCA gym. He set as the ol of the game the tossing of the ball into the basket— h, of course, gave the game its name. (Ladders were] ilongside the baskets to remove the ball after each § As a further refinement, he required the players noi n with the ball. Instead, they had to advance the ʼward the basket by dribbling, or bouncing, the they ran.

This new of basketball quickly became very popular in S d. From Springfield it spread around the country iughout the world. Over the follow- ing years, t of rules was accepted, the number of players eam were standardized at five, and in 1906 the iooden peach basket was replaced by an oper op hung with netting.

TH

B

f

Jaismith did not view basketball as a con- ː he did realize that some overzealous play- rough in the heat of a tightly contested game. ited that a penalty be imposed on any player ʲved, held, tripped, or kicked another player. ɹation is called a foul. When a foul occurs, the who is fouled is given a free throw at the basket. ɪayer who is fouled while shooting is given two free ows.

To realize how far basketball has come from its non-violent past to today, consider the following incidents that occurred in less than two months during the 1987–88 season:

December 7, 1987. At the Cornell University–Syracuse University game in Syracuse, player Greg Gilda of Cornell and Derrick Brower of Syracuse began bumping and shoving each other and were soon exchanging punches. Derrick Coleman of Syracuse joined the fray, and all three were thrown out of the game.

January 19, 1988. When longtime college rivals La Salle and St. Joseph's met in Philadelphia, the St. Joseph's mascot—a student dressed in a hawk costume—started to flap its wings during a time-out. Three men on the La Salle cheering squad—including 6-foot-8-inch, 250-pound Rodney Blake—jumped on him to make him stop, which led to their ejection from the arena.

January 22, 1988. Pat Cummings of the New York Knicks and Michael Cooper of the Los Angeles Lakers wrestled each other to the floor during a game in Los Angeles. Each was fined $5,000 and suspended for one game.

January 27, 1988. At a game between Towson State College and Rider College, Dwayne Martin of Towson State and Jim Cleveland of Rider began trading punches. After they were separated, Cleveland landed one extra kick on Martin, which led to a full-scale melee involving both teams, their benches, and some 400 fans. The game was stopped at that point, and Martin and Cleveland were suspended for two games.[7]

Most fouls occur in the heat of the game while players are shooting or struggling to grab the rebound off the hoop or backboard. While jumping with arms raised, the players are in a poor position to protect themselves. All eyes are on the hoop. This is a perfect opportunity for someone to poke an elbow into an opponent's face or stick a sharp knee into his groin—hoping that the referee will not see it. The dig is invariably followed by a look of complete bewilderment and "Who me?" innocence on the face of the perpetrator as the victim drops to the floor doubled over in agony from a broken nose, split eyebrow, eye injury, or some other painful hurt to the body.

The body parts to be injured most frequently in basketball are the nose and eyes. Multiple fractures of the nose are not at all uncommon. Dave DeBusschere had his nose broken three times, Willis Reed five times, and Jerry West thinks eight times but says it happened so often that he just lost count. After sustaining two serious eye injuries, Kareem Abdul-Jabbar of the Los Angeles Lakers began wearing welder's transparent plastic goggles to protect his eyes during the game.[8]

Some of the roughest play in professional basketball involved the Syracuse Nationals about forty years ago. The single game with the most fouls took place between the Syracuse Nationals and the Anderson Packers on November 24, 1949. Elbows and knees were flying throughout, and more time was spent in kicking, tripping, and slugging players than in playing basketball. At the end there were a total of 122 personal fouls—fifty-six called against Syracuse and sixty-six against Anderson. All ten starting players committed at least six fouls, which meant they were "fouled out" and had to leave the game.[9]

The record for fouling out was established by the Syracuse Nationals during their November 15, 1952, game against the Baltimore Bullets. A total of eight Nationals fouled out, and the referee had to allow some players to return to the game so that Syracuse could field a team of five men.

The most fouls in a play-off game came on March 21, 1953, between the Syracuse Nationals and the Boston Celtics. The two teams accumulated 106 fouls between them, of which Syracuse contributed fifty-five and Boston fifty-one. In the course of the game, seven Syracuse and five Boston players fouled out.

The Syracuse Nationals set another record on March 12, 1956, when Dick Farley fouled out after just five minutes in a game against the St. Louis Hawks.

COMBAT ON THE COURT

As we have said, most of the violence that occurs in the course of the game results in foul calls. The player who suffers the violence is given one or two free shots, and then play resumes. But the violence does not always end there. Sometimes, the angry feelings escalate into a fistfight or a melee that can involve the players on the court, the players sitting on the sidelines, and the fans. This eruption can either interrupt the game or, in some rare cases, bring it to an end.

A number of sorry spectacles stand out among the many that have occurred in recent seasons. Perhaps the most famous was the time that Kareem Abdul-Jabbar of the Los Angeles Lakers broke his right fist throwing a powerful straight punch to the head of Kent Benson, who was then playing with the Milwaukee Bucks. Among the very strangest incidents was probably the 1984 scrap between two stars of basketball, Larry Bird of the Boston Celtics and Julius Erving of the Philadelphia 76ers. What made this event especially startling was that Bird and Erving were close friends off the court!

The cause of the violence between Bird and Erving was probably the great pressure to win. A lot was riding on this particular game. It was early in the season, and both teams came to the contest undefeated. At one point near the end of the third quarter, Bird had the ball and Erving was effectively blocking a shot when a foul was called against Bird for elbowing Erving. The two men started trading insults until Erving suddenly lunged forward and grabbed Bird by the throat. This quickly turned into a boxing match between the two. Within seconds, the two benches had emptied and teammates on both sides had joined the fracas.

As soon as order was restored, referee Dick Bavetta did the unexpected. He threw the two most celebrated players of the day out of the game! Later, Bird and Erving were each fined $7,500 by the NBA, and fines totalling $15,500 were levied against the sixteen other players who had joined in the brawl.[10]

The most notorious violent incident occurred during the 1977 season. The villain was Kermit Washington—6 feet 8 inches tall and weighing 230 pounds—of the Los Angeles Lakers. Washington was known as an "enforcer," a rough and tough player, whose job it was to scare and intimidate—and perhaps injure—the opponents. In the course of a game with the Houston Rockets, Washington got into an altercation with the Houston center, Kevin Kunnert, which soon had the two men slugging it out.

Rudy Tomjanovich, Houston's best ballplayer, who had never been in a basketball fight in his eight years on the team and who was known as a peacemaker, dashed forward to pull the two apart. As he approached at full speed, Washington turned and smashed him full in the face with a single powerful punch. Tomjanovich fell to the floor with many bones in his head completely crushed and his face forced out of shape. His nose, jaw, and several bones in his skull were broken. In addition, he suffered a brain concussion, extensive lacerations of the face, loss of blood, and leakage of spinal fluid from the brain cavity.

The doctors wired Tomjanovich's jaw into position and performed three operations to repair all the damage. Tomjanovich suffered intense pain for months after the injury. One doctor later commented that he had never seen a victim of a car crash who looked worse than Tomjanovich did after that single punch!

Washington later said, "I hit him instinctively. I had no idea who it was. I just saw him coming at me and swung. Now that I've talked to other people, I understand Rudy wasn't going to fight. It was an honest unfortunate mistake." Mistake or not, Tomjanovich sued Washington for $2.6 million. The jury, in an extremely rare decision, raised the award to $3.3 million.[11]

Basketball violence is not confined to one sex, however. It has now become a part of women's basketball as well. A famous example is the January 17, 1987, game between the University of Oklahoma Sooners and the University of Missouri Tigers. The violence started just twenty-four seconds before the end of the game. Missouri player Lisa Ellis was fouled by Margaret McKeon of Oklahoma, whereupon Ellis flung the ball at McKeon's face. Both players had fouls called against them, and the game continued to the end.

After the game, the two teams shook hands, as is traditional. But the Oklahoma coach took that occasion to lecture Ellis for her unsportsmanlike behavior on court, waving her finger in the young player's face. Ellis pushed the coach's hand away, and the violence erupted again! Someone grabbed Ellis from behind. She fought back. In seconds, the players and coaches from both teams were entangled in a huge mass of kicking, punching, and shoving bodies. Fortunately, there were no serious injuries.[12]

THE COACH'S ROLE

"Defeat is worse than death because you have to live with defeat." So wrote Jim Musselman on the locker room wall when he became coach of the lackluster University of Minnesota basketball team, the Gophers. Coach Musselman made it very clear from the start that he wanted a winning team. He insisted that his players approach every game with as much determination and aggressiveness as was necessary to win. And he stressed that he didn't care what they had to do to gain victory. Hurting some of the other team's players was, therefore, acceptable behavior.

The Musselman approach seemed to work. The Gophers played well and intimidated their opponents to the point of winning all four of their opening games of the season. Finally, they were up against the powerhouse team, Ohio State, with its outstanding star, Luke Witte. Ohio State, led by Witte, piled up a big lead over the Gophers and seemed about to clinch the game when, thirty-six seconds before the final whistle, two of the Gopher players managed to knock Witte to the floor, punching him in the head as he fell.

As Witte started to rise, one Gopher offered him a hand as though to help him up. But instead, he held Witte's hand while viciously kneeing him in the groin. Witte collapsed again. This time, another Gopher player left the bench, walked over to Witte, and deliberately kicked him in the face. The kick unleashed a free-for-all, with Gopher fans storming onto the court and attacking all of Ohio's players.

This bestial expression of gratuitous violence, which was seen on television, outraged the nation. The governor of Ohio described it as a "public mugging." *Sports Illustrated* called it a "cold, brutal attack, governed by the law of the jungle." But Luke Witte's father, a professor of philosophy, didn't blame the University of Minnesota athletes. "As far as I'm concerned," he said, "the entire situation traces back to the coach, Bill Musselman. Musselman's intent seems to be to win at any cost. His players are brutalized and animalized to achieve that goal."[13]

Coaches do not only encourage violence in their players. Often, they also whip up the fans into frenzied activity. In fact, much of the fan violence and rioting of the 1976 NBA championship series between the Boston Celtics and the Phoenix Suns is thought to have been due to Celtics coach Tom Heinsohn. By nature a highly excitable man with a volatile personality, Heinsohn challenged every decision that was called against the Celtics. In one game before a very partisan Boston crowd, he ranted and raved so loudly that the people in the stands, who had been drinking rather heavily, streamed onto the court attacking the Phoenix players as well as the officials.[14]

FAN VIOLENCE

Quite often, it doesn't require an overly dramatic coach to lead spectators at a game to commit acts of violence. Team loyalty is also a major cause of basketball violence off the court. Just to mention a few egregious incidents:

In 1965 in Detroit, eight people were stabbed right after a game in a high school basketball tournament. The following two games were played without spectators so as to avoid any further violence.[15] So many fistfights broke out among fans of two rival Rochester, New York, high school basketball teams that no one was admitted to any of their games for a month in 1984.[16]

Five people were arrested, one man's face was slashed and required forty stitches, and one policeman was injured in a riot at the 1988 Martin Luther King Classic, a basketball tournament between New York City and Long Island high schools that was held in the Nassau County Coliseum in Uniondale, New York. The coaches and game officials blamed the fracas on the rap group Public Enemy, which had appeared earlier in the evening, shouting obscenities, carrying plastic machine guns, and working the crowd up to a fever pitch of raucous excitement. But the promoters of the event insisted that the cause was the intense rivalry between the city and suburban schools.[17]

Six bystanders were slightly wounded outside a dance party in Eastport, New York, just after midnight on February 28, 1988. The injuries resulted from a shotgun duel between two rabid high school basketball fans—one a loyal supporter of the Riverhead High School Team, the other an equally devoted follower of their rivals from Bellport High School.[18]

THE SITUATION TODAY

Basketball has come a long way from the peaceable game that Dr. Naismith envisioned back at the Springfield YMCA. What happened?

Here are a few possible explanations of what may have contributed to the change:

Some teams—at professional, college, and high school levels—have found that they can win more games through intimidation than by building a reputation as good players who just want to sink basketballs and avoid on-court fisticuffs.

The stakes are bigger now. Some college and high school basketball teams earn significant sums of money for their schools. And professional basketball has become truly big business, with million-dollar TV contracts and six-figure salaries. The difference between a winning and a losing season can translate into many thousands of dollars for the people involved. With that much at risk, some players are willing to use any tactics that will help them to win.

One sure way to gain the attention of coaches and professional scouts is to be the scrappy player on the team. Aggressive members often stand a better chance of getting an athletic scholarship to pay for their college education and later of getting a job offer from a professional team. And a successful career has the added bonuses of personal adulation and widespread media exposure.

A reputation as a violent team sells more tickets to the games. Many fans are drawn to games that have a strong likelihood of fistfights or player brawls. Spectators fill the arenas or gyms, buy more beer and hot dogs, and thus bring larger sums of money to the team owner or the school. Because many team owners and coaches realize that "violence pays," they don't try too hard to hold back the players. Even the referees now tend to call fewer fouls than they did in the past.

Some say that the game invented by Dr. Naismith is beginning to bear a slight resemblance to a game played by the Mayan Indians in Mexico thousands of years ago. In the Mayan game, the teams tried to pass a solid rubber ball through a large vertical ring set in a high stone wall. No one knows how much violence there was in the playing of the game, but one thing is certain. As soon as one team got the ball through the ring, the captain of the winning team cut off the head of the defeated captain!

Is this the direction we are headed? What can the NBA do to stem the tide of violence?

Among the suggestions that have been made are the following:

- Continue fines of $5,000 or more for instigators of violence. Even for highly paid athletes, $5,000 is a lot of money. The league could also decide to double the fine for subsequent incidents.

- Give more suspensions so that the players would not be able to participate in a number of games. This would be an even greater deterrent; it would probably antagonize the ticket-buying fans and the coaches, but it might discourage violence. No one interested in basketball wants to see a game with a key player out of action.

- Toughen up league rules against flagrant fouls and adopt a three-referee system to cut down on altercations.

The costs of these changes would be high. But it might be money well spent. If it saves just a few players from being permanently injured or perhaps even killed, it is indeed a small price to pay.

CHAPTER

BOXING AND WRESTLING

- "I am going to punish him. I am going to beat him so badly that he'll need a shoehorn to get his hat on again," said Cassius Clay [Muhammad Ali] before his fight with Floyd Patterson in 1965.[1]

- "When the surest way to win [a sporting event] is by damaging the opponent's brain, and this becomes the standard procedure, the sport is morally wrong," says Dr. George D. Lundberg of the American Medical Association.[2]

- "They pay me to get them in trouble," said Sugar Ray Robinson after he killed Jimmy Doyle in a welterweight title fight.[3]

- "The evidence for both brain damage to boxers and increased violence in spectators is overwhelming. The impact from any one bout may be small, but the overall impact on both the boxers and society is quite harmful," says Dr. Thomas Radecki, psychiatrist.[4]

Boxing is the only sport in which the main object is to hurt the opponent. In all other sports, the violence is incidental to the central goal. Of course, violence may occur while advancing the ball to the goalposts in football, trying to get the puck into the goal cage in hockey, or attempting to sink the ball through the hoop in basketball. But violent acts are not legal, approved of, or applauded as they are in boxing.

Though very violent, boxing in America is a legitimate sport. Serious injuries occur all the time, no matter what safety measures are taken. Reforms now being called for may be steps in the right direction. But there is a growing movement to outlaw boxing altogether. Many believe that as long as this sport exists, tragic instances of injury, disfigurement, and death will continue.

HISTORY AND BACKGROUND

The earliest evidence of fighting as a sport dates back to ancient Egypt some 5,000 years ago. From material found in old tombs, it would seem that men fought in bouts that were all-out combat, combining elements of what we now call boxing and wrestling. Although boxing began in Egypt, it was the ancient Greeks who took up the sport with the most enthusiasm. They even made boxing part of the very first Olympic Games.[5]

One innovation introduced by the Greeks was to wrap thongs of leather or cloth around the fighter's fist, hand, and forearm. The purpose was both to protect the bones and to increase the power of the blows. The Romans later modified this wrapping into what they called a *cestus*. The *cestus* consisted of a wrapping like that used by the Greeks. But embedded in the *cestus* was a heavy metal weight. Of course, this added tremendous force to every punch and turned the boxer's fists into even more deadly weapons.

Around the sixth century B.C., the Etruscans in Italy started to include fights in their funeral rites for the wealthy and famous. In the ceremonies, slaves were forced to fight to the death in front of the laid-out corpse. The purpose was to ensure that the departed one would enjoy a good afterlife.

The greatest boxer of ancient times was probably the Greek hero Theagenes. He is described as the undefeated champion from 484 to 468 B.C. Legend has it that he won 1,400 championships, each involving the defeat of a number of challengers, fighting some at the rate of ten a day! It is also reported that he killed some 800 opponents using his fists alone.[6]

As time went on, boxing became increasingly bloody—and deadly. The main instrument for this change was the *murmex*. This devilish device added a sharp metal spike, or several spikes, to the *cestus*. With the *murmex* a single blow could be fatal. Many fights were decided with just one punch. Whoever succeeded in landing that first blow almost always was declared the winner. Slaves, criminals, and prisoners of war were forced to fight using the *murmex*. Survivors of these bouts might later be pitted against wild lions.

So horrendous had boxing become during the days of the Roman Empire that in the year A.D. 500, Emperor Theodoric abolished it as a sport.[7] This ban lasted until around 1700, when boxing became legal again, this time in England. The usual form was for two fighters to stand toe to toe along a chalk line drawn on the ground and to pummel each other with their bare fists. Neither fighter was allowed to retreat or try to avoid the blows. Each kept hammering at the other until one of them fell to the ground. At that point, the other fighter flung himself on top of the hapless victim. Using his thumbs, he gouged the opponent's eyes, and with his hobnailed boots dug into the flesh until he was declared the victor.

The leading British fighter of the eighteenth century was Jack Broughton. In 1743, Broughton promulgated a series of seven rules that set minimum sportsmanlike standards of fairness and compassion for boxing matches. Broughton's rules were replaced in 1867 by the Marquis of Queensberry rules, which ushered in the modern era of boxing. Among the significant features of the Queensberry rules were fixed-length rounds, rest periods, and a ten-count to signal the end of the fight.

Toward the end of the nineteenth century, padded gloves were introduced and became standard for all boxing matches. Curiously enough, the purpose was not to protect the face or body of the person on the receiving end of the punches. Rather, they were to protect the fists of the boxers throwing the punches, since the bones in the fingers and hand break much more easily than the larger bones in the face.

The basic rules of boxing are very simple and have changed little over the years. Two men, of approximately the same weight, are placed in a square ring (called ring because in ancient times fights took place in round arenas) that measures about 20 feet on each side. Each fighter has the same basic goal: to land punches on his opponent and defend himself against the opponent's punches.

There are four fundamental types of punches. The straight right is the most powerful punch in the boxer's arsenal. One study reported that such a punch has a force sixty times the force of gravity and lands at a speed of about 30 miles an hour![8] The jab consists of a short, sharp, straight, stinging blow. An uppercut is a punch that is thrown upward from around waist level. And a hook is delivered in an arc with a bent elbow.

The bout is divided into three-minute rounds with one-minute rest periods between rounds. Most fights last for ten rounds, most championship bouts for fifteen. The fight can end in one of three ways. The first and most damaging is the knockout (KO). Medically speaking, a knockout is a concussion, or brain injury, caused by a blow to the head hard enough to cause a loss of consciousness. For the knockout to end the fight, the period of unconsciousness must last at least ten seconds.

A fighter who is unable to score a knockout will try to land enough blows on his opponent's head and body to make him too hurt, too dazed, or too weak to continue. Sometimes, this is done by hitting the opponent in such places and in such ways as to cause bleeding, which can also lead to victory in the ring. Most top fighters are so strong and well trained, though, that they keep on fighting even when barely conscious.

It is up to the referee, the third man in the ring, to decide if the injured fighter can adequately defend himself. If not, the referee stops the fight and declares the other boxer the winner by a technical knockout (TKO). Should neither fighter score a KO or a TKO, then the bout goes the full number of rounds. Most boxing matches have two judges who score the fight along with the referee. The winner of any round gets 5 points and the loser from 1 to 4 points according to how well he fought. If a round ends in a draw, each boxer gets 5 points. The winner is determined by a decision of the referee and judges based on the total number of points they give to each boxer.

BRUTALITY
IN THE RING

One fight that may best point up the inherent violence of boxing is the March 1962 Benny Paret–Emile Griffith fight at Madison Square Garden in New York City. In the twelfth round, Griffith had Paret backed against the ropes that surround the ring. While Paret lay twisted in the ropes and unable to defend himself, Griffith continued his attack. He landed eighteen powerful blows to Paret's head before the referee decided that Paret had, in fact, been knocked out. A few days later Paret died of the beating he had taken in the ring.[9]

This is one extreme example among many hundreds that show the damage that results from punches to the head in the boxing ring. The blows that are thrown in a professional prizefight are powerful indeed. A straight right by a good heavyweight boxer strikes with a force of 10,000 pounds! Basically, this sort of punch in the head causes the brain to bounce around within the solid, hard bones of the skull. The first result is a temporary loss of consciousness, lasting less than a minute.

The greater danger is what happens when the brain collides with the skull. Just the sheer force of the impact crushes and destroys brain cells. At the same time, though, some of the small blood vessels in the brain break. Blood leaks out. The only place it can go is the narrow space between the brain and the skull. As more and more blood fills this gap, it builds up the pressure on the brain tissue. This is called a hematoma. If the hematoma is mild, the result will be the destruction of more brain cells. If it is a severe hematoma, death can follow.

The number of deaths directly related to boxing—either in the ring or soon after a fight because of injuries sustained during the fight—is staggering. There have been around 500 deaths just since 1900. A 1980 study of boxing deaths during the period from 1970 to 1978 found that there were an average of twenty-one boxing-related deaths every year. This study was based on a survey of 5,500 boxers and shows a rate of 3.8 deaths per 1,000 participants. For comparison, there were 1.3 deaths per 1,000 participants in college football and 0.1 deaths per 1,000 participants in high school football.[10]

How does the number of injuries in boxing compare with the injuries in other sports? In 1984, the National Safety Council released figures showing that 50 percent of all boxers experience some sort of injury. Football is next, with a 30 percent injury rate. But the other sports are way lower, with baseball at 3 percent, basketball at 2 percent, and the others lower yet.[11]

A strange confrontation between a boxing death and the law occurred in Australia in 1884. In a legal, sanctioned boxing match, James Lawson floored Alex Agar with a powerful punch over the left eye. Agar was taken to the hospital but died before he arrived. Because of the terrible outcome, Lawson was accused of manslaughter. A jury found him guilty and sentenced him to a prison term of six months.[12]

Most victims of death in the ring are lesser-known fighters—men who don't have the skill, strength, speed, or stamina to protect themselves or to survive a beating. But over the years some top-flight champs and contenders have been killed in prizefights:

In a 1947 battle for the welterweight crown, Sugar Ray Robinson killed Jimmy Doyle.[13]

Leading lightweight challenger Ray "Boom Boom" Mancini killed Duk Koo Kim in their 1982 title bout.[15]

The following year, former featherweight champion Barry McGuigan killed his opponent "Young Ali" from Nigeria.[16]

Not long after, Francisco "Kiki" Benjines died in a bantamweight title bout with champion Alberto Davila.[17]

Perhaps the only boxing death that can be said to have benefited humanity in some way was that of Charles Mohr, the star of the University of Wisconsin boxing team. Mohr died of complications that resulted from a 1960 fight. He sustained the fatal injuries despite the fact that he was wearing a head protector. The uproar following his death led directly to the ban on college boxing that is still in effect today.

The jarring and shaking of the brain within the skull—in part from single knockout blows, but even more from the many lighter blows every fighter takes during his career—also damages many structures of the brain. This leads to a condition known to doctors as boxer's encephalopathy. In popular talk, the boxer has become "punch-drunk." The obvious symptoms of the condition are slurred speech, an unsteady, shuffling walk, mental confusion, hand tremors, memory problems, and such personality disturbances as extreme aggressiveness, depression, and paranoia.

Apart from the brain and nervous system, the rest of the body also takes a terrible beating. Cracked ribs, broken noses, and cauliflower ears are frequent occurrences in the world of boxing. Perhaps the best-known example of physical abuse occurred during the longest fight in history on April 6, 1892, in New Orleans. Andy Bowen and Jack Burke slugged it out for seven hours and nineteen minutes, a total of 110 rounds! When it was over, observers commented that the faces of both boxers looked like raw hamburger meat.[18]

One of the earliest scientific studies of boxing violence was concluded by Dr. A. H. Roberts in London in 1969. He examined 224 boxers and found that thirty-seven (16.5 percent) were punch-drunk, with twelve (5.3 percent) severely affected. Two years later, Dr. J. Jedlinski studied sixty amateur boxers in Poland and discovered that 50 percent had suffered some neurological damage. Eventually, five had to be hospitalized.[19]

Dr. J. A. N. Corsellis is a leading expert in boxing injuries. In 1973, he performed autopsies on the brains of two former world champion boxers, ten professional boxers, and three amateurs—all of whom had shown signs of being punch-drunk. In every case, he saw actual structural damage to the brain. And he also found evidence that the harm was not due to a few superpowerful KO punches but rather the result of a steady shower of lesser blows to the head.[20]

The following year, Dr. Corsellis asked 165 other British neurologists how many athletes in all sports they had treated with symptoms of punch-drunkenness. Over one twelve-month period, these doctors had seen twelve jockeys, five professional soccer players, two amateur rugby players, two professional wrestlers, one sport parachutist, and 290 boxers!

During the 1980s, a number of different researchers studied the brains of living boxers. They found evidence of permanent brain damage in between 50 and 87 percent of those studied.[21]

Muhammad Ali, one of the outstanding heavyweight champions of recent years, is a classic example of a fighter who suffered the effects of brain damage from many years of boxing. In his youth, Muhammad Ali was a fast, strong, classy fighter, with a sharp mind and a real way with words. But by the time Ali finally retired in 1979 he showed few signs of the man he had been. He displayed many characteristics of a punch-drunk fighter, with difficulty in speaking, a slow, staggering walk, and problems in expressing himself. Doctors diagnosed his condition as Parkinson's disease and blamed it on the cumulative effect of the many blows he took to his head during his long boxing career.[22]

BOXING-RELATED VIOLENCE

Boxing violence is not confined to the ring; it seems to permeate everything connected with the sport. Take the 1951 world middleweight championship bout in Berlin, Germany, between the champ, the American Sugar Ray Robinson, and the German challenger, Gerhard Hecht. Halfway through the first round Robinson landed a hard left hook to the body that sent Hecht to the canvas writhing in pain. The very partisan crowd became enraged at the thought of an American—especially a black American—knocking out a German. The referee, Otto Nispel, counted to nine, and then, in an unprecedented move, announced that he was pausing one minute. Before the minute was up, the bell rang ending the round. Hecht staggered to his feet and hobbled to his corner.

Hecht was not very steady on his feet when he came out for the second round, and the flurry of lightning punches that Robinson unleashed soon had him down again. Robinson went to a corner awaiting the count, confident that he was about to be declared the winner. But to his shock and disappointment, Nispel ruled that Robinson had thrown a foul punch below the belt. The decision went to Hecht.

The exultant German fans were on their feet at once rejoicing and roaring "Foul! Foul! Foul!" Ecstatically they flung beer bottles and all sorts of trash into the ring. "What's the matter with you?" Robinson demanded of the referee. "You know that wasn't a foul!" To which Nispel replied, "I have to call it a foul. I want to leave this ring alive!"[23]

Perhaps the biggest eruption of fan violence followed the defeat of the so-called White Hope, Jim Jeffries, by the first black heavyweight champion, Jack Johnson, in Reno, Nevada, on July 4, 1910. Expecting an outbreak of racial violence, officials searched all spectators entering the fighting arena for guns and other weapons. None were found, and the fight took place without incident. But no one was prepared for the rash of violence that shook the entire country right after the fight when a group of armed blacks took over the town of Keystone, West Virginia, and held it for twenty-four hours; three blacks were killed in a gun battle with whites in Uvaldia, Georgia, and two were stabbed in Muskagee, Oklahoma; major riots were reported in Arkansas, Colorado, Maryland, Mississippi, Missouri, Ohio, and Pennsylvania; and the U.S. Marines had to be called out to restore order in Norfolk, Virginia. All told, in the days after the Johnson-Jeffries fight, nineteen persons were killed, 251 injured, and about 5,000 arrested![24]

David C. Phillips, a sociologist at the University of California, San Diego, made a study of the rate of homicides in the United States following highly publicized heavyweight championship fights. His method was to survey the records for the three weeks following each of the eighteen title bouts held from 1973 to 1978 and to compare them to the norms for the same years.

The results were quite interesting. Phillips found that there were 193 "extra" murders after those fights as compared to the norms. That works out to be a 12.46 percent increase after each fight, with the greatest jump occurring within the first three days. The largest single increase came after the Muhammad Ali–Joe Frazier fight on October 1, 1975, when the murder rate shot up over 32 percent. According to Phillips's theory, people see how violence is prized in the boxing ring and come to believe that violence outside the ring will also be rewarded.[25]

THE FUTURE OF BOXING

"Professional boxing is hopeless and doomed to meet the same fate in the United States that it has met in Sweden and Norway: extinction." So wrote Dr. George D. Lundberg in an editorial in the *Journal of the American Medical Association* on May 9, 1986.[26] Since then, the AMA has been joined by the medical associations of Canada, England, and Australia, the World Medical Association, the American Academy of Pediatrics, and the American Academy of Neurology in calling for the abolition of boxing as a sport.

By some standards, other sports, such as football, auto racing, hang gliding, mountain climbing, and ice hockey, might be considered more dangerous. Still, boxing arouses the most heated discussion and the most agitation for a complete ban. It may be because violence is the main object of boxing. As Joyce Carol Oates put it in her famous book *On Boxing*, "The brain is the target, the knockout the goal."[27]

By now, nearly everyone recognizes that boxing almost inevitably results in permanent brain damage or death. What, then, are the arguments against a ban?

One line of defense stresses the value that boxing has for the individual competitors. It is said that the intense physical training develops the body, gives the individual a good sense of self, and teaches the athlete the value of discipline and hard work. Preparation for the sport also provides valuable lessons in determination, self-control, and tenacity. The value of sports in building character is widely held, but a good argument can be made for developing the same qualities through participation in other sports, ones that do not have the same tremendous potential for damaging the mind as boxing.

Another view is that every individual in a democracy has the freedom to make his or her own choices and that this basic right should not be subject to government interference. Adults who choose boxing fall into that category, supporters say. But just as the government insists that drivers and passengers in automobiles wear seat belts and that motorcyclists wear helmets in order to save lives, so boxing's opponents insist that the government has the authority to ban boxing as a way of saving lives.

Some hold that boxing is an escape valve, both for the fighters and the spectators; it is a way to get rid of pent up rage and belligerence. Without boxing, they claim, there would be more violent crime in the streets and even more wars between nations. Studies that have been done over the years have failed to provide any evidence for the position. On the contrary, innumerable research papers show what seems to be a "causal link" between watching boxing and engaging in real-life aggression.[28]

Perhaps the most popular argument in defense of boxing is that the sport offers a very positive way for young minority, deprived, or ghetto men to make their way out of poverty and to add hope to otherwise dead-end lives. But this view, too, has not been supported by any hard evidence. Very few fighters ever reach the point of making a living from boxing, and many more are felled by injuries that stop their careers from developing. The odds are very much stacked against anyone following this road to success. Getting an education and developing technical and business skills is a much more likely way of escaping poverty than boxing, critics say.

Besides working to ban the sport, what can be done to minimize the dangers of boxing? Some doctors in the AMA find themselves in a strange position in this matter. They support the boxing ban yet believe ways must be found to improve the sport and protect the health of the boxers so long as boxing is still legal.

Some experts have come up with proposals that might be helpful. One general idea is to allow boxing to continue but to change the rules. Among their specific recommendations are the following:

Disqualify blows to the head. Since most of the serious, lasting damage is done to the brain, this will add a measure of protection to that vital organ.

Wire the boxers so that punches could be counted and measured electronically. Just as sword-fight killings of the past have been transformed into the highly skilled sport of fencing, so boxing could be changed from injury-inflicting brawling into ritualized fisticuffs that rewards skill and speed more than brute force.

Ban boxing gloves. This would help in two ways: It would reduce the impact of punches, since the fighter's hands perspire in the gloves, adding weight and making the gloves more like clubs to beat the opponent. Also, it would reduce the number of punches thrown, since the finger and hand bones are so fragile that fighters would be afraid of breaking them.

Limit the lengths of fights. The longer the fight, the more punishment the boxers are forced to take, especially in the later rounds when they are tired and less able to defend themselves. Shorter fights will preserve the excitement of the sport but without exacting so cruel a toll on the participants.

Although boxing critics have proposed mandatory protective headgear, most medical experts are against this measure. The added weight and the irregular surfaces of the headpiece, they believe, would result in more head injuries, not fewer.

The best way to reduce the injuries from boxing may be the establishment of a federal governing body to regulate the sport. This group could require legal reforms, such as better and more complete physical exams before and after the fight and greater involvement of the physician during the fight itself. Also, a national registry of boxers would further protect boxers. Fighters with any sort of physical or neurological impairment would not be allowed to fight; boxers in general would not be allowed to fight too often; and they would not be permitted to fight too soon after a KO.

Only a national body could effectively ban the sport. Right now, boxing is controlled by the states. No state wants to be the first to stop boxing within its borders because it would lose the income that prizefights produce. In addition, there is little question that the fight promoters would sidestep the ban by simply moving the bouts to other states.

Since 1700, and the reappearance of boxing after a 1,200-year absence, the sport has steadily been undergoing reforms and changes that make it safer, more humane, and less violent. There is every reason to believe that such improvements will continue to be made. It is just as likely, however, that one day boxing will be banned altogether.

WRESTLING

All sports that attract onlookers must strike a balance between athletics and entertainment. Wrestling, as seen in college and high school wrestling meets, is mostly athletics. The meets that are held offer most observers little in the way of exciting action, overt show of physical strength or skill, or excitement. Few people would pay to be spectators at these competitions.

Professional wrestling is another story. It has chosen to emphasize the entertainment side of the sport. A match is more a theatrical performance than an athletic contest. But wrestling does have its dark side. The show is usually violent, the ring a "theater of violence." Although the outcome may be preset, the moans, groans, and cries of pain exaggerated, and the injuries apparently less serious than they appear, there is still plenty of risk and danger to competitors.

Some British wrestlers recently described the kinds of injuries that they sustained in the ring:

George Kidd: "I have two cauliflower ears and I'm deaf in one of them. I've had broken ribs, a broken nose and have a torn tendon which made one calf permanently smaller than the other."[29]

Les Kellett: "I had one injury where the bone was split lengthwise from the wrist to the elbow. I've had my ankle broken, and I was in the hospital for four months with two operations to remove abscesses on my back caused by body slams and falls."

In the words of wrestling promoter Mike Judd: "Bert Asserati was probably one of the greatest wrestlers ever, a fearsome man. Now he is a cripple—walks on two sticks, can only see out of one eye, joints all locked together. He's got everything wrong with him you could possibly imagine."

Many think that professional wrestling should also be banned, not only for the damage it does to the bodies of the wrestlers but also because of the harmful effect it has on many fans. As writer Ralph Schoenstein writes, "A so-called 'sport' whose players have such names as 'The Hammer,' 'Abdullah the Butcher,' 'The Samurai

Warrior,' 'Mad Dog Vachon,' 'Killer Kahn' and 'Killer Kowalski' is also novocaine for the soul."[30] Wrestling matches have been held responsible for inspiring people of all ages to act brutish and go out of control.

Of course, supporters of wrestling accuse opponents of overreacting to a form of entertainment that they consider harmless and hammy. The violence is faked, they insist, and the wrestlers are just pretending to punch and kick each other.

Though there may be some disagreement about whether professional wrestlers are athletes or actors, there is no disputing the fact that the sport does cause serious, permanent injuries. Is the American public willing to have the wrestlers suffer pain for their entertainment? The question needs to be answered. And the answer is up to all of us.

CHAPTER

FOOTBALL

- *"I wasn't going to tear his lips off. Maybe poke his eyes out,"* said Greg Townsend, Los Angeles Raiders defensive end.[1]

- *"Once you become friends, you feel like you can't hit them in the face, poke them in the eye or slam 'em or club 'em,"* says Ronnie Lippett, New England Patriots cornerback.[2]

- *"If I get a hand on you, I'm going to make you suffer. I'm going to punish you,"* says Terry Williams, New York Jets cornerback.[3]

- *"There's a lot of hitting just as the whistle blows and maybe some of it is a little late. I guess they pride themselves on hitting and hitting hard,"* says Rich Miano, New York Jets safety, speaking of the Houston Oilers.[4]

- *"Speed and quickness are great, but so is toughness, having the guts and courage to run into a guy going that fast,"* says Rusty Tillman, Seattle Seahawks coach.[5]

Football ranks among the most violent of sports. Yet it is one of the most popular sports. Thousands and thousands of fans jam the football stadiums at every game during the season. And many millions view the Super Bowl on TV each year.

Football is a highly physical, fiercely competitive contest between the eleven players on each team. The aggressive nature of the sport has a marked effect on participants and fans alike.

HISTORY AND BACKGROUND

Football is believed to have sprung from the Roman sport of *harpastum*. This game had two goals set at either end of a long field. The aim was to move the ball, believed to be about the size of a modern soccer ball, behind the opponent's goal line. The second-century Roman physician Galen described *harpastum* as a rough game that included much physical contact and relied heavily on tackling, running, and throwing of the ball. Presumably the Romans used the game as part of their military training, to toughen up the legendary Roman legions.

The Roman conquest probably brought *harpastum* to Britain, where the game came to be called "fote-ball." By 1175, the game had evolved into a rough kind of mob football that pitted village against village, town against town. The entire length of the town became the field, with the goals placed at opposite ends. The players followed few rules. Teams were very large, sometimes with over 500 young men, and the rough free-for-all usually lasted an entire day.

Because the game had no rules, it was permissible to kick an opponent or try to trip him. In fact, a player could do anything at all to get and keep the ball. Small wonder that many injuries resulted.

The first of many players to die from a football injury was Henry, son of William de Ellington, who was accidentally stabbed during a game in 1280. Less severe injuries were very frequent in those early days of football.

"Broken shins, broken heads, torn coats and lost hats are among the minor accidents of this fearful contest," wrote the historian Glover, referring to the "ruthless" Derby game. He went on, "It frequently happens that persons fall, owing to the intensity of the pressure, fainting and bleeding beneath the feet of the surrounding mob."[6]

A great deal of mayhem and violence resulted from this form of gang football. Many ordinary citizens and onlookers were hurt, and city streets and businesses suffered considerable damage. In 1314, the merchants of London obtained from the king a ban on future games. This measure was followed over the next 500 years by various other laws, passed by other English rulers, making it a crime to play football in England. King Edward II, for example, banned the game with a decree that read, "Football, wherein is nothing but beastly fury and extreme violence, wherefore it is to be put in perpetual silence."[7]

Despite the many bans and edicts, football continued to be a very popular sport in England. By the seventeenth and eighteenth centuries, more than forty separate communities throughout England got together once a year to play football. One notorious football match took place between the towns of Sheffield and Norton in 1793. The game lasted for three days and resulted in a huge number of casualties. For years after, it was considered unsafe to hold football matches in certain cities because the rivalries were so intense.

The Industrial Revolution brought with it a shift of population from country towns to city centers. This put an end to mob football. The modern form of the game began to emerge. It started in the schools of England and was chiefly promoted by the educator Thomas Arnold. Arnold considered the tactics—including the practice of "hacking," stopping an opponent by kicking his shins— a good way to build a boy's character. Under Arnold, football also became a way of training young men for the wars being fought by the British Empire. In fact, the same cries—"Charge!" "Kill 'em!"—were used in both football and battle.

By the mid-nineteenth century, football had become the most popular school sport. But over the years two sets of rules emerged. One set of rules—used at such schools as Rugby, Marlborough, and Cheltenham—allowed the ball to be carried by hand, and that game became known as rugby. And the other rules—used at Eton, Harrow, Westminster, and Charterhouse—allowed the ball to be advanced only by kicking, and that game became what Americans call soccer.

In both rugby and soccer many players were seriously hurt, and a few were killed; in addition, the fans fought and brawled as they watched the shifting tides of the games. Writer Don Atyeo called it "controlled violence" and said that the teams played "with a purpose better suited to war than sport."[8]

When the sport was imported to America, colleges such as Harvard and Yale chose rugby as the preferred version. And from this beginning, the game of American football evolved. From the start, though, the American form of the game was much rougher than the rugby on which it was based. "There is no 'sport' outside of a bullfight that presents the same degree of ferocity, danger and excitement as that shown in an ordinary intercollegiate game of football," wrote the *New York Tribune* in 1890.[9]

As the injuries mounted, the public asked that players be equipped with face masks, nose guards, shin pads, and leather helmets. The players at first objected to wearing the protective equipment, fearing that it would compromise their strongman image. But reluctantly they agreed on the necessity. Soon they found that the devices did more than free them from certain types of injury. They also gave them new ways to inflict damage on their opponents.

The football season of 1905 was particularly violent. Eighteen college and high school students died and more than 159 were seriously hurt on the football playing fields of the United States. One of President Theodore Roosevelt's sons, a freshman at Harvard, came home from the first day of practice with a black eye. The president became greatly upset by the high rate of college football injuries, and he threatened Yale, Princeton, and Harvard with a ban unless they changed some of the rules of the sport. At the president's urging, the flying wedge was outlawed as a move, and a neutral zone between opposing lines was set up. Roosevelt's demands to outlaw rough play also led to the legalization of the forward pass in 1906.

By the early 1920s, more reforms were instituted. Yet the violence continued to grow worse, even as the game grew more popular.

The origin of professional football also dates back to around 1920. Many college athletes were attracted by the huge sums that were being offered to professional players. Among them was Harold "Red" Grange, the famous "Galloping Ghost" of the University of Illinois football team, who joined the professional Chicago Bears. Grange was paid several hundred thousand dollars as a pro and earned much more for his team. His experience showed players and owners alike that football could be an extremely profitable sport.

PLAYER VIOLENCE

As football grew more remunerative, it also became increasingly violent. One measure of its violence comes from the estimates of football-caused injuries and deaths prepared annually by the National Collegiate Athletic Association. In the year 1987 alone, the sport killed four players and injured 329,987.[10] According to some medical reports, injuries reduce the life expectancy of a professional player by about twenty years. Even the players and coaches themselves are amazed by the violence of the game.

"It takes intestinal fortitude to run 40 yards at full speed and get in those tremendous collisions," said Rusty Tillman, coach of the Seattle Seahawks.[11] It has been calculated that the force of the collision between a fast-running 240-pound lineman and an equally fast-running 240-pound back is "enough to move 66,000 pounds, or 33 tons, one inch."[12] A hard hit on the helmet can approach a force of 1,000 Gs, which is a thousand times the force of gravity. This is roughly ten times the force that astronauts experience on takeoff!

From the very beginning young players hear their coaches tell them to "go out there and break someone's arm." Peewee footballers have been treated for concussions, and boys have been urged to charge each other and butt their heads together during training. There is considerable pressure on young football players to perform aggressively, with little regard for sportsmanship or the injuries they might cause. Many coaches try to instill a win-at-all-costs spirit in their players. The tactics, too often, may include spearing and illegal tackling—both of which can cause serious spinal injuries.

The injury statistics for high school, college, and pro football are quite startling. Here are a few:

- Each season at least fifty and as many as eighty-six out of every hundred high school football players receive injuries serious enough to keep them from playing for more than a week.
- About thirty-two college and high school students become paraplegics (paralyzed from the waist down) each year as a result of football injuries.
- Any boy who plays the game through high school and college has a 95 percent chance of serious injury.

- Of 108 freshmen football recruits at the University of Iowa over a four-year period, more than one-third had suffered serious injuries of the neck and spine while playing high school football.[13]

One 1988 survey based on detailed reports from 112 high school programs found that the number of major injuries rose more than 20 percent in two seasons, from 54,407 in 1986 to 65,634 in 1988. This comes to an average of about 4.5 major injuries (defined as those that keep a player out for more than three weeks) per team per season. Although these figures alarm some, others say that the increase could mean that high school football is getting safer; they claim that coaches may simply be keeping injured players out longer.[14]

The average career of a professional football player lasts just over four years—the shortest of all the professional sports. Not only does every player, whether in high school, college, or on a professional team, have a greater risk of serious injury, but each one can expect to be scarred for life. Some, like Citadel linebacker Marc Buoniconti, have their lives changed forever as a result of a football injury. Buoniconti tackled East Tennessee State running back Herman Jacob during a game on October 26, 1985. His spinal cord was badly damaged on the play, and he was left a permanent quadriplegic (paralyzed in both arms and both legs).[15]

A typical professional National Football League (NFL) player suffers 2.5 injuries every season. Four out of the twenty-two players on the field for every game are playing with a serious injury; five out of the twenty-two are playing with an injury that would put any other person out of action. Team members on the so-called suicide squad have eight times the rate of other players' injuries. Linemen suffer broken fingers and dislocated fingers. Concussions (ten or more during a career), shoulder separations, broken limbs, torn knee ligaments, and dislocated hips are not uncommon. One surgeon is said to have compared the strain of a body block to "the thrust of a railroad tie against the unsupported knee."[16]

Not all the injuries occur in the course of a play either. Some are the result of so-called extracurricular violence, or "cheap shots"—hits, kicks, butts, eye gouges, etc.— that the aggressive players sneak in when official play is over and when they think they will not be seen. A cheap shot is anything that will hurt or confuse an opponent— a lineman going on to flatten an opponent *after* throwing a block, a tackler bringing down the quarterback *after* he releases the ball, or a secondary whacking a pass receiver when his back is turned.

Why do players indulge in cheap shots? Some just get particularly vicious once they are on the football field. Others consider it part of the game, a tactic that they use to help them win.

Here are two striking examples of cheap shots:

Darryl Stingley, a wide receiver for the New England Patriots, tried to make a leaping catch of a pass in a preseason game with the Oakland Raiders on August 12, 1978. Stingley missed the ball, but immediately afterward Jack Tatum of the Raiders, nicknamed "The Assassin," slammed into Stingley and belted him in the head with his padded forearm. The blow literally broke Stingley's neck and instantly turned this twenty-six-year-old 6-foot, 195-pound superb athlete into a quadriplegic. Although the injury left Stingley unable to move, the referee didn't even call a penalty on the play![17]

Steve Largent, the Seattle Seahawk receiver, had to leave the 1988 season opener with the Denver Browns after suffering a brain concussion and two broken teeth. He was running for a pass but could not hold on to the ball. After the ball had fallen to the ground, Mike Harder, the Denver free safety, tackled Largent and gave him an extra hit in the head that caused the injuries.[18]

Although the record of injury and death would seem to be proof that the game is excessively violent and warlike, some players and coaches disagree. Assaults on the field are merely part of the game they say, and the tales of violence are exaggerated.

A recent game that shows how violent football has become was the September 18, 1988, contest between the New York Jets and the Houston Oilers. The Oilers came into the game with a reputation as the "bad boys" of football for their brawling, fighting style of football. The Jets felt that they had to prove themselves tougher than the Oilers in order to win. Before the game, Jet player Wesley Walker asked the coaches if the club would pay any fines that might be imposed for personal fouls in what promised to be a very aggressive game. "They said they would," reported Walker.

On the very first Oiler play, James Hasty, rookie right cornerback for the Jets, got involved in a shoving match with the Oilers' veteran wide receiver, Ernest Givins. "My intention was to get our team fired up," Hasty later explained. And it did indeed spark any number of violent incidents and scuffles that kept on erupting throughout the game.

The first Jet touchdown came after a pass reception by Kurt Sohn, who complained, "The second guy who came along tackled me after I scored, and he stuck his fingers in my face mask and tried to gouge my eyes."

In one fistfight, Ray Childress of the Oilers ripped the mask off Jets' player Reggie McElroy so he could land punches on the face. When asked what started the fracas, McElroy would not say anything more than, "I've never been that mad before in my life."

Jet receiver Al Toon was drilled by Oilers safety Jeff Donaldson and had to leave the game with a mild concussion and a lacerated lip.

At one point, Mark Gastineau raised his hand to the crowd, asking them to cheer after a touchdown. But when

Cody Carlson of the Oilers raised his hand mockingly in Gastineau's face, fists started to fly.

Jet Nuu Faaola jumped on Oiler Domingo Bryant on a punt return and started pummeling him—even though Bryant wasn't carrying the ball!

At the end, there were a total of twenty-one penalties—Jets eleven, Oilers ten—and nine personal fouls—Jets, five, Oilers, four. But the aggressiveness the Jets displayed worked; they won, 45 to 3. Perhaps the game was best summed up by the Jets left tackle, Dave Cadigan, who said, "I've never been part of anything like this before." [19]

Fans who attend games in huge stadiums are sometimes unaware of all the violence taking place on the field. Many of the hits and kicks thrown by the players are hidden from view beneath helmets, masks, and layers of padding. The athletes appear as virtuous as knights in armor, innocent and invincible. Television, too, distances the viewer from the action and softens the full impact of the violence. The full effect of the brutality, the groans and cries of pain, are seldom seen or heard.

American football provides almost limitless opportunities for violence, and in fact sometimes demands its use. As Harvard psychiatrist Chester M. Pierce said, "The coach must have his men feeling that they not only *can* kill but that they *should* kill." [20]

The rigorous training program for the football season is designed to toughen up the players and weed out the "softies." Drills are often long and abusive and include such activities as telling the players to run at full speed into a solid wall or tying two men together and urging each one to drag the other across the field. One college coach reportedly said that he ended a practice session only when he had seen blood.

At game time, coaches work very hard to get players into the right mental frame of mind to win. One college coach supposedly showed footage of war films before the game. "There is nothing stokes the fire like hate," said the legendary Green Bay Packer coach Vince Lombardi.[21] Alex Karras, retired lineman of the Miami Dolphins, said that he came onto the football field with hate in his heart for everyone and a completely changed personality. That attitude, he believes, was the only thing that kept him in the league.

During the football season, every player has to work up a rage that peaks on the day of the game. The methods of getting "psyched up" vary from destroying a locker room before a game to withdrawing from wives and families a few days before going out on the field. Those who have difficulty becoming enraged before games week after week may resort to alcohol or drugs to help trigger angry outbursts.

Many players have testified to the great amount of drugs used by footballers at all levels of the game, starting in high school. Amphetamines fight off weariness and deaden pain, and they also promote aggression. Football player Houston Ridge filed a suit against the San Diego Chargers, saying he was given drugs "for the purpose of stimulating mind and body so he would perform more violently as a professional."[22]

Some sports analysts believe that there is a direct relationship between the level of violence in football and the amount of drugs players take. Arnold Mandel, a Los Angeles psychiatrist, spent a season observing the San Diego Chargers firsthand. Mandel later reported, "The most important influence creating the violence in football—professional or college—is high-dose amphetamines. You actually become, for the peak effect of the drug, crazy. And it's the most murderous type of crazy that we know."[23] And on the other side of the coin, players who have reduced their dosage of amphetamines have been found to be less effective on the field because they are not as aggressive.

The NFL now forbids the use of drugs and insists

that drug use is currently very slight. In 1986, as part of their effort to remove illicit drugs from football, the league instituted drug-testing procedures for all players.

Few players appear out of control on the field. But as one player commented a decade ago: "If they say, 'It's not whether you win or lose but how you play the game,' then, fine, a lot less guys will use drugs. But they've never said that. And as long as winning is the name of the game, you have to take what you can."[24]

In July 1987, Lawrence Taylor, star of the New York Giants, revealed that he used cocaine often and that the Giants' management and the NFL knew of his drug problem. The head coach of the Giants, Bill Parcells, said in his autobiography that from 1983 to 1986 he knew of twenty to thirty players on the team who had used drugs. Some, he said, were still with the team.[25]

FAN VIOLENCE

Fights in the stands at football games are now frequent occurrences. So are obscene chanting and the flinging by spectators of beer cans, toilet paper rolls, ice, and all other sorts of trash at opposing players. Some of the missiles are thrown just to annoy. But others are thrown in the hope of wounding a player or injuring an opposing fan.

Some experts think that such fans are after power. If the team is number one, their backers are also number one. But if the team is losing, both players and hometown fans feel frustrated and angry. Such feelings can easily boil up into a rage, and the target of the fury becomes the visiting team and its supporters.

One particularly long-lasting and rough rivalry exists between the students of the Colorado School of Mines and those at Colorado College. Since 1899, there has been tremendous tension at the annual game held by the two teams.

In the old days, the winners would celebrate their

victory by using dynamite to blow up the rival's goalposts. And it was an act of uncommon bravery for a Colorado College student to venture anywhere near the School of Mines. It has been said that any Mines' students who caught a Colorado College guy on campus during the week before the game would burn an *M* on his forehead with nitric acid!

The 1920 game was probably the most violent that the two colleges ever played. Just about every student from both schools was present, and at half time they all poured down onto the field to do a snake dance. It was inevitable that the two lines would collide—with disastrous effects. The second half of the game had to be delayed while dozens of police struggled to separate the combatants and find enough stretchers and ambulances to cart away the wounded.

Ever since then it has become a yearly tradition for the fans to swarm onto the field at half time and after the game and to chase the students from the opposing school. Bloody noses, black eyes, and many more-serious injuries are the order of the day. The emergency room at the local hospital is always prepared for the scores of wounded that arrive throughout the afternoon.

Psychologist Jeffrey H. Goldstein speculates that the violence between football fans is not so much the rivalry between colleges or between cities but the result of aggressive instincts being aroused by the game itself. In 1971 Goldstein did a study comparing the hostility in spectators before and after a college football game and before and after a gymnastics competition. He found that the hostility increased rather considerably for the football fans but that there was virtually no change in the audience for the gymnastics match. Also, he discovered that the increase in hostility occurred no matter if the onlooker was rooting for the winning or the losing team.[26]

That football is a violent sport for both players and fans is now widely accepted and documented. In a study on sports-related injuries of school-age children, conducted by Dr. Basilius Zaricznyj of the Southern Illinois University School of Medicine, the researchers found that football causes the highest percentage of injuries, 19 percent, followed by basketball at 15 percent and baseball at 10 percent.[27]

Dr. Joseph S. Torg, director of the University of Pennsylvania Sports Medicine Center, is a leading expert in head and neck injuries sustained by football players. He found that one of the biggest causes of such injuries was the use of helmets as battering rams by some players. Tackling or blocking with heads lowered frequently caused serious injuries both to the tacklers and blockers and their targets. Dr. Torg passed his finding along to those who control high school, college, and professional-level football. Action came very quickly. Rules were passed forbidding players from using their heads and helmets to butt other players.[28]

Tighter rules and regulations have reduced somewhat the number of deaths and serious injuries from football, yet it still remains a highly dangerous sport. Besides the free-for-all on the gridiron, there are numerous fights, scuffles, and shouting matches in the stands. All considered, the violence is sometimes so considerable that it makes the fast-paced and thrilling game of football hard to enjoy.

CHAPTER

ICE HOCKEY

■ *"Fighting is part of hockey," says Gerry Cheevers, coach, Boston Bruins.*[1]

■ *"I kind of like going out, bumping guys. I'll instigate through aggressiveness," says Mick Vukota of the New York Islanders.*[2]

■ *"I was just doing my job," said Dave Brown of the Philadelphia Flyers, after cross-checking Tomas Sandstrom in the head, sending Sandstrom to the hospital with a brain concussion.*[3]

■ *"When you're playing for the Stanley Cup, you've got to learn to take and give a hit," said Brian Propp of the Philadelphia Flyers, after receiving a brain concussion and lacerations of the temple, lip, and scalp.*[4]

■ *"We have a very violent, emotional game and things are going to happen," says Brian O'Neill, executive vice president of the National Hockey League.*[5]

Perhaps the best capsule view of hockey violence comes from one day's injury roster of the New York Rangers. The date is November 11, 1987:

Maloney—rotator cuff problems; out for two weeks.
Sandstrom—finger fracture; out for ten days.
Froese—dislocated shoulder; out for ten days.
Larouche—back strain; out for seven days.
Greschner—knee problems; day to day.
Ogrodnick—bruised tail bone; day to day.[6]

Many injuries that occur in ice hockey are accidental. They happen because of fully legal actions of the game, such as checks (bumps against their opponents) and body slams (pushes onto the boards) by players moving at speeds of up to 30 miles per hour. In addition, as each player tries to get the puck into the goal cage, other players are sometimes struck with the stick, hitting with a force of 72 foot-pounds, or the flying puck, traveling at around 120 miles per hour.

Along with the many accidental injuries that occur are a number that are deliberate and malicious. The use of sticks as weapons is an accepted part of the game. So, too, are the pushing, grappling, and punching matches that take place all the time. Owners and managers seem to feel that fighting to let off steam is healthy. Apparently, the fans agree. Ticket sales have never been better.

HISTORY AND BACKGROUND

Ice hockey is a fast game played by two six-men teams on an ice-covered rink. The origins of this sport and that of field hockey go back thousands of years to the cultures of the ancient Chinese and early American Indians. The various forms of the game they played were all based on the principle of hitting an object—a piece of wood, a stone, or a soft ball of animal hair covered with buckskin—toward a goal of some sort.

The more modern version of hockey arose in the British Isles, where variations of the same game were called bandy in England, shinty in Scotland, and hurling in Ireland. In all these games, the object was to hit the ball with a curved stick, sending it either to a teammate or toward a goal.

Ice hockey probably was first played by British soldiers stationed in Canada during the mid-1800s. The soldiers were serving with the Royal Canadian Rifles at Kingston, Ontario. Looking for a way to amuse themselves during the long Canadian winter, they adapted the sport from ones they had at home—field hockey and ice skating.

The soldiers probably made up the game as they went along. After sweeping the snow off the ice-covered harbor at the rear of their barracks, they tied "runners" to their boots and began hitting a ball around with borrowed field hockey sticks.

The first recorded use of the term "ice hockey" was in connection with a match that took place at the Victoria, Canada, Skating Rink in 1875. The popularity of the game quickly spread, but there were problems. A hard rubber ball on the ice proved impractical; it jumped about too much and traveled too fast. The teams were either too large or too small. And the goal was often nothing more than a line. Without uniform rules, every group played the game differently.

McGill University in Canada set up the first standardized set of rules for the game in 1879. Eventually, the number of players on each side was fixed at six. The goal line was replaced by a net, and the ball was replaced by a puck, which McGill players were said to have first cut out of a solid rubber ball.

In 1893, to encourage the spread of the game, Lord Stanley of Preston, governor-general of Canada, originated a trophy, called the Stanley Cup, to be given each year to the outstanding team. At that time, virtually all players were amateurs. But, as the game grew, clubs began to hire professional players. These men wanted to be able to compete for the trophy, too. Stanley had not fore-seen this possibility, and the professionals soon crowded out the amateurs. From 1913 on, no amateur team has won the cup, a prize that has come to symbolize the top team in the world of professional ice hockey. It has been awarded since 1926 to the playoff winner of North America's National Hockey League (NHL).

Ice hockey arrived in the United States in the early 1890s. The sport became so popular that Americans began to speak of it simply as hockey. Basically, players move up and down the rink on ice skates striking the puck with a curved stick. The skaters try to score goals by knocking the puck past the goalkeeper and into a goal cage. The goalkeepers dive and slide about in front of their cages to try to stop shots from reaching the goal.

Players move the puck down the ice with their sticks. Defending players try to get the puck away from the attackers by checking (slamming them with their bodies), blocking them with their sticks, or intercepting the puck.

The referee controls the game and calls fouls on players who hold opponents, strike or slash with the stick, or abuse the officials. A foul can result in a penalty, which means that the player has to sit in the penalty box at the side of the rink for as long as ten minutes. While a player is in the penalty box, his team continues to play with fewer men on the ice. More serious incidents may lead to a multiple-game suspension for the player (twenty is the maximum thus far) and a fine.

Hockey has always had outrageous incidents of violence. Faces have been slit open by skate blades, heads have been smashed by sticks, shoulders have been separated by body checks; and innumerable fistfights have erupted among players and spectators alike.

One of the early casualties was the Canadian professional skater Owen McCourt, who died in 1907 after being hit by an opponent's stick. The player believed to have delivered the blow, Charlie Masson, was arraigned on a murder charge but then was acquitted because no one could positively identify him as the one who struck McCourt![7]

The National Hockey League was formed in 1917 to regulate this exceedingly rough sport. By 1925 or so, one player, Eddie Shore (known as the Babe Ruth of hockey), had become particularly noted for his fierce behavior on the ice. His name is now permanently identified with hockey violence.

Shore once charged player Ace Bailey during a match. He lifted Bailey up with a body check that sent Bailey somersaulting through the air before landing on his head. While Bailey lay on the ice, legs twitching, Shore grinned. Bailey required two brain operations and many months of bed rest to recover from this incident.

The many injuries he suffered in the course of his career left Shore scarred for life. Among his hockey wounds were fractures of his hip, collarbone, and back, along with a broken jaw five times, a broken nose four-teen times and, over the years, the loss of every one of his teeth! In addition, a total of 978 stitches had been sewn to close some eighty lacerations—a record that still stands today.[8]

Some of the injuries Shore sustained no longer occur today with the same frequency. The NHL has made hel-mets and face masks for the goalies mandatory. Although the headgear seem to have reduced injuries somewhat, they are not very popular. Most professionals do not want to be thought of as "sissies" in what they consider an ultra-macho sport.

GRATUITOUS VIOLENCE

More than any other sport, hockey has developed a rep-utation for being much more violent than is absolutely necessary to play and win the game. Few attempts have ever been made to limit the most damaging forms of hockey violence—high sticking (raising the stick above shoulder level), charging into other players, slamming a person into the boards, digging with the elbow, spearing or slashing with the stick, and tripping, or cutting, with the skate. Players still get their teeth knocked out, their jaws broken, and suffer brain concussions with such regularity that such violence is now almost considered routine.

It is only recently that there has been any real effort to reduce fistfighting. Indeed, some still excuse this form of violence, saying that it is a harmless way for players to release their frustrations and tensions. But many people doubt that the fights spring from the "frustrations" of the game. As Dave Brown of Philadelphia explained: "I don't know if I ever really get all that mad. You have to have a clear head when you fight. You don't want to be swinging wildly. You try to aim at the nose or the chin, someplace where, if you land one, it'll cause damage. Broken nose, broken jaw—that's the quickest way to get the point across. There's no sense getting into a fight if you're not trying to hurt them."[9]

Some hockey coaches actually promote the violence. They train players to crash their way through lines of opponents and teach them ways to improve their fighting skills. They urge their players to use violence to achieve specific purposes—to think of assault on the ice as a "skill" rather than a "sin," as sociologist Robert Faulkner suggests.[10]

A player builds his reputation among opponents, teammates, and fans alike by acting tough. He is always testing himself and others through threat and insult. The worst thing a player can do is give in, back down, or run away from a fight. Nothing can bring him down faster in the eyes of others than being considered weak or timid.

The cardinal rule for every player is to come to the aid of a teammate at the first sign of distress. Whenever a fight breaks out, the player must honor the "buddy code." This means he must either prevent opponents from joining in or must move in himself. Anyone who fails to do this lets the other player know that he is not someone who can be trusted. Once his teammates lose confidence in a player, that player's days on the team are numbered.

Even children's hockey leagues across North America encourage players to be "gutsy." Having guts means that the player is willing to fight if provoked. It means that he is able to take cheap shots and to fight "like a man." "Retaliate with your fists," children are told, "and, if possible, with the butt of your stick. Show that you want to win the game and that no one can push you around."

Coaches also get embroiled in ice violence at times. On Valentine's Day, 1985, Detroit Red Wings coach Nick Polano and Minnesota North Star coach Glen Sonmor started to brawl at the end of the first period. Fortunately for them, Monte Clark, former coach of the Detroit Lions, was in the stands. Within seconds, 6-foot-6-inch, 270-pound Clark dashed down and pulled them apart, saying sagely, "You hockey people are crazy."[11]

Some people claim that hockey today is less violent than football. They support their position by citing statistics that show hockey players suffer far fewer severe injuries than football players. But this may not tell the whole story. In hockey, both the thrower and receiver of the blow are sliding around on their skates. Therefore, the blow does not land with nearly the force of blows thrown when both parties are standing on firm ground. However, when the number of penalties in each sport are tallied, hockey seems to be the most aggressive sport.

THE ESCALATION OF HOCKEY VIOLENCE

An upsurge in hockey violence began after 1967. In that year, the number of existing NHL teams was doubled, and six more teams were added. With expansion came a new intensity in the game. New teams were willing to fight especially hard to survive. Some of these clubs found themselves short on talent and experience, with only guts and nerve going for them.

In some ways, the Philadelphia Flyers were typical of these so-called expansion teams. When they started, the Flyers lost almost every game. A new coach, "Ferocious" Fred Shero, was brought in. He helped them develop a new set of winning tactics. As he said, he put "hitting back into hockey."[12] Led by Dave "The Hammer" Schultz, the Flyers began to win games through intimidation, brutality, and a determination to avenge all real or imagined wrongs against any of their players. The Flyers under coach Shero ushered in the era of what has come to be called "goon hockey."

The Flyers, on their way to the Stanley Cup championship in 1974, tallied a total of 1,756 penalty minutes—600 more than the next most-penalized team. Shero brainwashed the Flyers with such proverbs as "If you can't beat the other team in the alley, you can't beat them on ice." As coach, he put his team through some brutal drills. For instance, one player was assigned to stand in front of the goal while two others tried to mug him. The victim was supposed to show how tough he was by keeping them from breaking the bones in his body.[13]

As the Flyers became a winning team, other teams followed suit. Schultz later commented, "That's how I made the league, by fighting. And I've had to fight to stay here."[14] Shero said the same thing about Shultz. "Speed, skill, and strength make a hockey player," said the coach. "Schultz realizes he does not have speed or skill, so what is he here for? To beat up the other guy."[15]

Largely as a result of Schultz's behavior, the NHL adopted some new rules. These rules barred head butting and the taping of fists. Penalized players had to move directly to the penalty box without brawling on the way. A number of incidents became court cases in which the violent players were charged with aggravated assault and other crimes. Several players were found guilty, fined, and in some cases suspended from playing.

One trial involved with hockey violence took place in 1975, when Boston's Dave Forbes was charged with aggravated assault using a dangerous weapon. In this case it was his hockey stick. His victim was Henry Boucha of the Minnesota North Stars. Boucha was left with a fractured eye cavity, twenty-five stitches, and double vision after Forbes attacked him with his stick following a scuffle on the ice.

Forbes testified that Boucha had hit him with a "sucker punch" from behind, and that he felt he had to retaliate or Boucha would think "He could walk all over me." In his own defense, Forbes said that fighting back is an integral part of the game, taught to players from the very beginning. The trial ended with a hung jury and no verdict.[16]

At the trial, Boston coach Don Cherry explained that he felt a lot of pressure before the game because of a losing streak. He believed that his job was on the line. "It has always been my philosophy," he said, "to win at all costs."[17]

As a result of outcries to reform the sport, the NHL took further action. In 1976, they introduced the "aggressor rule," which mandated a five-minute penalty for any player starting a fight along with possible expulsion from the game. The new regulation resulted in the suspension of eleven players in the 1977–78 season.

Of course, violence continues to pervade ice hockey, even though some feel the character of the violence has changed. Brian O'Neill, the NHL's executive vice president, shares this belief. "It was not an uncommon thing in those days [the last decade] to see two players stand up and swing sticks at each other," he said. "You don't see that much anymore. What you see are the quick slashes."[18]

Still, at least one controversial incident of violence comes to Mr. O'Neill's attention each week. It is his job to rule on such incidents and mete out appropriate punishments. He is in the odd position of being employed by the owners and being the man in charge of disciplinary action against the players. Some who would like to rid the sport of unnecessary violence would prefer an independent body or person to handle suspensions, someone or some panel that has nothing to do with the NHL. They feel that O'Neill will hesitate to suspend any of the stars of the game, since they are the ones who attract the large crowds. But, at the present time, the final ruling is up to O'Neill.

A ruling against a player begins with a call to the NHL and a referee's report of any possible incident of hockey violence. A video tape arrives soon after this; after viewing the tape, O'Neill decides whether or not to hold a hearing. If he decides a hearing is needed, he invites the player, along with officials and representatives of the player's club, to gather in the NHL offices. O'Neill reviews the reports and plays the tape for the player. The player has a chance to explain his actions in the rink. After the hearing, O'Neill reviews the evidence and gives his decision within twenty-four hours. In the 1987–88 season, O'Neill suspended twenty-two players for excessive violence or for abusing an official.

O'Neill has been criticized for being too lenient and inconsistent. He admits the difficulties of being objective. "Every case is different," he says. "You have to deal with the intent of the players, the severity of the action, the extent of the injury, the premeditation, the provocation." [19]

Often O'Neill's decisions are bitterly criticized. In the 1987–88 season, he drew disapproval from many who thought that his suspension of Dave Brown for fifteen games after his vicious attack on Tomas Sandstrom of the Rangers was not tough enough. At the same time, Cliff

Fletcher, general manager of the Calgary Flames, thought O'Neill was unfair when he ordered Gary Suter to miss four NHL games for an incident that occurred in international play.

FAN VIOLENCE

Former NHL president Clarence Campbell learned the hard way what can result from taking an unpopular action against hockey violence. Campbell suspended Montreal's star forward, Maurice "Rocket" Richard, from the 1955 playoffs for fighting. The action wounded the pride of French Canadians everywhere, and mayhem resulted.

When Campbell arrived at the Detroit-Montreal game in Montreal on the evening following his decision, the French Canadian fans pelted him with a barrage of programs, peanuts, eggs, fruit, and overshoes. At intermission, a smoke bomb went off. In the panic, many of the 14,000 spectators stampeded out of the stadium. Once outside, they tore down trolley lines, overturned and burned cars and newsstands, looted stores, and fought with police for seven hours. Over a hundred people were arrested before tear gas dissipated the crowds.[20]

A 1979 game between the New York Rangers and the Boston Bruins ended with the disappointed New York spectators throwing food and garbage down on the ice and screaming at the Boston players. But violence broke out when a fan reached over the railing and punched Boston's Stan Jonathan. The Bruins attacked the fans and fought with them until the police moved in. Four Ranger fans were arrested, and three Boston players were suspended for a total of twenty games and fined $30,000.

What would fans do if violence were taken out of hockey? Would they continue to flock to the games? Would the excitement and quality of the game suffer?

In 1988, the *New York Times* polled a number of hockey fans on their feelings about violence in hockey. Several respondents who opposed the violence held the NHL responsible to some extent:[21]

"The NHL will never stop stick-swinging or any other ice-violence," one said. "The problem is money-related. The owners' money, in the form of player investments, is involved."

Another said that the violence would go on forever. "The NHL concern is not the red cuts and black eyes of the players, but the green dollars of the people paying to see the brawls and cheap shots."

Some hockey enthusiasts came up with suggestions on how the NHL could cut the violence:[22]

"Suspend or double the number of games that the victim is forced to miss as a result of the injury."

"Put in an all-or-none penalty, whereby a player found guilty receives a penalty of a certain number of games, with repeat offenders receiving more."

"Tighten the rules and eliminate the violence."

The many injuries sustained by the players and the reactions of at least some of the fans indicate that perhaps the time has come to put an end to the excessive violence of today's hockey—without losing any viewers or diminishing the excitement of the sport. In recent years, the Olympics and the Canada Cup hockey matches have proven that hockey can be a fast, thrilling sport that need not depend for excitement on seeing men knocked unconscious or lying in pools of their own blood on the ice.

CHAPTER

MOTORCYCLING AND HORSE RACING

■ *For several years, there have been Friday-night amateur motorcycle races just outside of Paris. Hundreds of young drivers compete, and 2,000 or more spectators come to watch the mayhem. In the last five years, sixteen drivers and onlookers have been killed accidentally and nearly 400 injured.*[1]

■ *In a 1973 horse race in California, jockey James Felton hit his archenemy, Rudy Campas, three times with his whip as they entered the stretch. Campas then grabbed Felton by the collar and yanked him off his horse. As Felton fell, his foot got caught in his stirrup, and he grabbed on to Campas's saddle. He was stretched between the two horses until Campas let go and Felton fell to the track. The wind was knocked out of him, but miraculously he suffered no other injuries.*[2]

■ *On October 14, 1988, 200 racetrackers gathered to mourn the death of Michael Venezia, the forty-three-year-old jockey who was killed in a race a few days before. Venezia either jumped or slipped off the horse he was riding after the mount broke a leg. The jockey fell into the path of another horse, who kicked him in the head, killing him instantly. Although investigators ruled that what happened was unavoidable, such accidents are bound to occur on the racetrack.*[3]

Motorcycling and horse racing are high-risk, exciting sports. They are also among the most exceedingly well-organized major sports anywhere. Motorcycling is governed by the American Motorcycle Association (AMA), which rules and regulates every phase of motorcycle activity, including safety. In horse racing, state racing commissioners supervise racetrack operations and oversee all races. Popular in all parts of the world, these two very daring sports attract millions of enthusiastic viewers to live and televised races wherever and whenever they are held.

MOTORCYCLE RACING: HISTORY AND BACKGROUND

It is believed that Gottlieb Daimler, the great auto pioneer, invented the motorcycle in 1885. His idea was simply to add a motor to the then fairly new bicycle, which had come into being around 1880.

But motorcycles remained little more than bicycles with motors until 1900 or so. That year, a bicycle race was held in New York City's Madison Square Garden. A motorized bicycle, powered by a small gasoline engine, was used to pace the riders. George M. Hendee, a well-known bicycle maker, was in the audience. He soon lost interest in the cyclists he had come to see but was fascinated by the motorized bicycle. Before the day was over, he had struck a deal to design and manufacture the first true motorcycles.

A few years later, in 1907, William Harley and three members of the Davidson family started producing motorcycles. These marvelous machines soon captured the imagination of people all over the world. Racing on motorcycles became a popular sport, here and in Europe.

Starting in 1914, however, World War I brought the sport of motorcycle racing to a standstill in the United States. Americans were much too involved with producing guns and tanks to bother with the new-fangled motorcycle. The invention even lay dormant through the postwar years as American automobile makers developed the assembly lines that turned out tremendous numbers of inexpensive cars. Americans loved the automobile to the exclusion of the motorcycle, and the motorcycle lost much of its allure. But in Europe the story was quite different. Cheap, mass-produced cars were not as widely available, and the motorcycle—and motorcycle racing—continued to grow in popularity.

In the mid-1940s, after World War II, interest in the sport began again in America. A severe worldwide shortage of gasoline and difficulty in getting the metal and parts to build automobiles made motorcycles a good solution to transportation problems. Soichiro Honda in Japan provided a big boost to the sport when he decided to produce and export motorcycles. Soon, motorcycles and motorcycle racing were back in the United States once again.

A MAJOR SPORT

Motorcycle racing—whether on a paved track or road or across fields of earth, mud, sand, or grass—is now a major sport, second only to auto racing in number of paid admissions. But like auto racing, it is the source of much violence. Many accidents and injuries occur to both drivers and spectators.

Take as an example the motorcycle racer Phil Read. Read, who captured the world championship eight times, suffered fractures of his back, collarbone, legs, ankle, arms, fingers, and pelvis. Whenever he was racing, his wife had in her bag the equivalent of over a thousand dollars in cash. "You never know when your man will have an accident and you'll need to pay cash for a specialist or a private plane to get him home," she explained.[4]

Barry Sheene, Read's closest rival, also had a staggering list of accidental injuries. These included four fractures of his left ankle, three fractures of his left wrist, two fractures of his right ankle, and single fractures of his right wrist, both legs, both collarbones, two fingers, nine ribs, and a forearm, along with seven compression fractures of vertebrae in his spine. Of course, the catalog does not include all the cuts, scrapes, bruises, and lacerations that are part of every motorcycle accident.

Sheene's description of the time he fell off his motorcycle while traveling at nearly 180 miles an hour in a race at Daytona is especially graphic: "I could feel the skin coming off my shoulder as I slid along . . . Everything hurt. I could feel all this hot stuff running down my back. It was blood. I could see blood all around me on the ground . . . I went to take off my glove and my wrist was bending three inches above where it should bend."[5]

Of all the motorcycle races around the world, the most dangerous and violence-filled is the road race on Great Britain's Isle of Man. The route, a 38-mile winding course, goes along a road filled with sharp turns and twisting curves, over mountains and through valleys. The drivers wing their way at speeds of around 200 miles an hour past brick buildings, fences, and telephone poles that tightly line the way. In the first seventy-four years in the Isle of Man race, 124 riders have been killed. The deadliest day came in 1978 when five riders and two spectators lost their lives in one huge, bloody crash.[6]

No discussion of motorcycling would be complete without a mention of the daredevil Evel Knievel. Although he was not primarily a racer, Knievel was a competitor who earned a very good living attempting thrilling, death-defying tricks and stunts with his motorcycle. The fact that he has failed in some of his more outrageous attempts would seem to indicate that these were indeed legitimate efforts, not just easy tricks made to look hazardous.

Take Knievel's feats during the year 1974. First, he

attempted to use his motorcycle for a jump across the Snake River canyon—and plummeted to the bottom. Only the emergency parachute that was attached to his bike saved him from a certain death.

Next, he went to England, where he jumped over thirteen London doubledecker buses—and crashed down on the landing ramp at 90 miles an hour, the impact throwing him under his bike with a fractured hand and damaged spine.

After recovering, he went on to Chicago and jumped across a shark-filled tank, where a bad landing again sent him to the hospital.

One can appreciate the extent of the damage that Knievel inflicted on himself by noting the sales pitch of an Evel Knievel doll that appeared in the 1970s. The tag described the doll this way: "It does everything that Evel does except go to the hospital."[7]

HORSE RACING: HISTORY AND BACKGROUND

The first horse race probably took place soon after humans first domesticated the horse some 5,000 years ago. These early races most likely involved two horses who ran side by side from one point to another; their owners were probably the first jockeys.

By 1100, the English had discovered that horses from Arabia and Morocco could run much faster than the horses in Great Britain. They began importing these Arabian and Moroccan mounts to the English countryside and used them for racing and breeding fast racehorses. All thoroughbreds are descended from these original mounts. The first racetrack was built in England around 1170.

Steeplechasing is a form of horse racing in which the horses jump over fences, some with ditches or pools of water on the other side of the fence. The sport developed from that of racing hunting horses across the countryside, which was popular in Britain as early as 1600.

Thoroughbred racing uses mounts with bloodlines that can be traced back to the famous stallions mentioned earlier. The sport became popular in the United States after the Civil War. The Kentucky Derby, the most famous horse race in this country, was first run in 1875. By 1900, it had developed into an exciting spectator sport.

Horse racing is also an extremely profitable sport. States collect millions of dollars a year by taking the bets that people place on each race. The profits are shared by the state, the track owners, and, of course, the bettors, with the racetrack usually taking more than anyone else.

The so-called Triple Crown of racing in the United States is made up of three separate races: the Kentucky Derby, the Preakness Stakes, and the Belmont Stakes. Perhaps the most famous winner was Citation, who ran in 1948. Other famous races are the Ascot Gold Cup in England and the Prix de l'Arc de Triomphe in France. Australia has the Melbourne Cup; Ireland, the Irish Sweeps Derby; and South Africa, the Durban July Handicap.

"OFF AND RUNNING"

Horse races usually take place on a flat, oval track made of sand, topsoil, and clay. Occasionally, the track is grass-covered. The length is usually a mile around, and the distance is measured in one-eighth-of-a-mile stretches, or furlongs. A typical race varies from 5 to 10 furlongs.

Most horse races are held during the course of an afternoon. Eight or nine races take place about thirty minutes apart. In between times, the spectators may pick the horses they believe will win and place bets. Trainers and jockeys saddle the horses and get them ready for the next race.

The jockeys are small, usually weighing 115 pounds or less, to keep down the weight the horses carry. The leading jockeys often earn higher salaries than most other sports figures. At the call from the track judges, "Riders up," the jockeys, in their colorful blouses and caps, mount their horses.

A bugler sounds the notes that call the horses to the post. The bugle call also lets spectators know that the race is about to begin. Jockeys sometimes gallop their horses for a short while to loosen them up before walking them into the stalls of the starting gate. When all is ready, the starter presses a button that unlocks the gates and rings a bell. "They're off," the track announcer shouts.

During the race, loudspeakers blare out the position of each horse in the race. The excitement mounts as the horses approach the finish line. Cameras automatically photograph the entire race. Sometimes the finish is so close that a horse may "win by a nose," and a judge, who closely supervises the race, must study the photos of the finish to decide the winner.

The Jockeys' Guild was formed in 1940 to promote improved safety standards and working conditions for the riders. Nevertheless, since they were organized, more than a hundred riders have been killed in accidents at U.S. tracks, and nearly fifty have sustained permanent injuries. During 1977 and 1978 alone, eight jockeys were left paralyzed and two were killed.[8]

The death of forty-three-year-old jockey Michael Venezia in 1988 was perhaps typical of most horse racing accidents. Venezia was riding the horse Mr. Walter K. at Belmont Park in New York. During the race, the horse stumbled and broke a leg. The mishap sent it lurching to the side and into the path of another horse, Drums in the Night. Venezia was thrown from the saddle, and before the jockey on Drums in the Night could react and change his course, Venezia had been trampled to death. Mr. Walter K. had to be destroyed because of its broken leg.[9]

To add to the risk of accidental death or injury caused by hurtling around the track at speeds of nearly a mile a minute atop about a half-ton of galloping horseflesh, there is the violence of jockey against jockey. Probably the low point came in the 1933 running of the great American horse race classic, the Kentucky Derby. Because of the deplorable behavior of two jockeys, that particular race is now commonly called the "Dirty Derby."

The two jockeys involved were Don Meade and Herb Fisher. Meade was an outstanding rider but very rough in competition. He was on Broken Tip, an underdog in the race. Fisher, who was not very well known or very successful, was on a favorite, Head Play.

For the first half-mile of the race, Head Play had the lead and Broken Tip was far behind, as had been expected. Then Meade began to move Broken Tip up from ninth place. Soon he was challenging Fisher for the lead. To maintain his advantage, Fisher tried to crowd Meade against the rail. Meade grabbed at Fisher's saddle cloth, as a way of warning him to keep away. But instead of heeding the signal, Fisher tried to push Meade off his mount.

By now the two horses were thundering down the final stretch. Since Meade could not be forced off his horse, Fisher grabbed hold of the jockey and started beating him with his whip—even letting go of the reins of his own horse. Meade stayed focused on the race, however, and was able to bring Broken Tip in a scant nose ahead of Head Play.

No sooner had they crossed the finish line than the enraged Fisher stood up in his stirrup and began beating on Meade. After the two riders were finally pulled apart, Fisher lodged a complaint with track officials. He claimed that Meade had won by interfering with his horse. The officials suspended both jockeys for thirty days.

Still seething over his loss, Fisher waited for another opportunity to assault Meade. The chance came when both men were in the jockeys' room. Fisher attacked Meade again, this time with a bootjack. For this act of aggression, he received an extra five days' suspension. Although both riders continued racing for thirty more years, they never again exchanged a single word.[10]

CHAPTER

SOCCER AND RUGBY

■ *April 1989. Ninety-five fans lose their lives and over a hundred suffer injuries as people push and shove their way into a soccer game in Sheffield, England.*[1]

■ *June 1988. During a week of matches for the European soccer championship in various cities in West Germany, more than 700 people are arrested for fighting and rowdyism.*[2]

■ *October 1986. In a London tube station, rampaging fans of the Millwall soccer team stab to death Ken Burns, age nineteen, for shouting "Up West Ham," the name of his favorite soccer team.*[3]

■ *May 1985. Thirty-nine are killed and more than 400 injured in a riot at a soccer match between a British and an Italian team in Brussels, Belgium.*[4]

■ *January 1971. Fans in Glasgow, Scotland, trample sixty-six persons to death when they try to return to the stadium they have just left upon hearing that a last-minute goal has been scored.*[5]

Soccer violence is unique in one way. Only in soccer is the violence among the fans before, during, and after the game greater than that among the players on the field!

Although soccer is probably the best-loved sport in many nations of the world, it has not caught the interest and attention of Americans to the same extent. Although soccer is slowly becoming more popular here, most accounts of soccer violence still come from Europe and from South and Central America, because that is where the most loyal and demonstrative soccer fans are found.

Soccer matches attract huge crowds of up to 200,000 people. The threat of violence at and around such matches, particularly in England, the Netherlands, Italy, and West Germany, and in a number of South and Central American countries, is great and ever-present. The violence varies considerably from nation to nation and from team to team. Some clubs are notorious for the hooliganism of their followers. Others attract far less troublesome crowds.

Because of the history of violence associated with soccer, officials now prepare in advance for the arrival of fans. People attending matches today often find the soccer stadiums ringed by mounted police. Helicopters hover overhead, and "hoolivans" equipped with closed-circuit video monitors cruise the area. In some places fans must carry identity cards, and the team owners must pay for armies of police to patrol the sports grounds.

Most women and children fear the violence at soccer matches and stay away, as do many upper- and middle-class families. As a result, the soccer fans found at these events are mainly young, working-class men. Many are unemployed. They come together to support their soccer teams but also to find an outlet for their anger and frustration.

HISTORY AND BACKGROUND

Soccer, or football, as it is called in England, became accepted in many English schools in the early 1800s. The

English football tradition insisted that the ball only be kicked or butted with the body; handling a ball was strictly banned. Occasionally, the code was enforced in an odd sort of way. For example, players were sometimes made to wear white gloves and hold a silver coin to prevent them from using their hands.[6]

For years the rules of the game varied. To get a consensus on how the game should be played, the English football clubs held a meeting in October 1863. A motion was adopted to form the Football Association. From an abbreviation for the term *Association* (Assoc) came the term soccer. As we said, though, in Great Britain the game is still called football.

In a soccer game, two teams of eleven players each try to knock a round ball with feet, head, or body into the opposing team's goal. The team that scores the most goals wins the game. The goalkeepers are the only players who may touch the ball with their hands. Skilled soccer players perform acrobatic leaps to advance the ball with their heads or turn and twist in midair to kick the ball in a different direction. The standard soccer uniform consists of shirts and shorts, heavy, knee-length socks, and cleated soccer shoes. Some players, in addition, wear shin guards.

Once the game gets under way, the players run up and down the field almost continuously. Play stops only when a goal is scored, a foul occurs, or a player is seriously injured. Once a player leaves the field for any reason, he cannot play again in that game. For this reason, soccer players often remain on the field in spite of painful injuries.

Soccer was the only form of football played in the United States until the 1870s, when American football came into vogue. During the 1920s and 1930s, soccer became a favorite pastime all over the world. In 1930, a Frenchman, Jules Ramet, presented a cup to the winner of an international competition. The competition, now held every four years, is called the World Cup. The winner is chosen by a series of matches between national teams from many countries.

BRITISH SOCCER VIOLENCE

Violence at soccer matches has occurred for a century or more. But of all nationalities, the British seem to have the largest share of "soccer hooligans"—a relatively new phenomenon. As Loda Walgrave, a professor of criminology at Leuven University in Belgium, said, "All the lines lead back to British hooligans. They are seen as the professionals. They are the great example for hooligans from all over the rest of Europe."[7]

The first targets of soccer violence were the British Rail's special football trains that carried team followers to and from the game. Fans going to the match or riding home broke windows, tore out seats, and smashed hundreds of light bulbs. In 1975, Liverpool fans looted the mailbags that were carried on the train and used them to set the rail cars on fire. Today, trains known as soccer specials are patrolled by police and occasionally by guard dogs.

Much violence occurs hours before the game has even begun or while the fans are still miles from the grounds. In Derby, England, for example, homeowners who live adjacent to the stadium board up their homes the night before a match. Police stay on the alert for youths who are out looking for trouble and for the violence fans inflict on each other and on any nearby property. In other places, police set up video cameras on the roofs of some of the houses near the stadium to spot and identify offenders on the street.

As game-time approaches, officers frisk almost everyone who enters the stadium, especially those who have paid low admission fees to stand on the terraces—huge concrete steps in front of the more expensive seats. Occasionally, the police search those headed for seats in the stands as well. They have found that many fans now arrive at the games carrying weapons. The list of weapons that have been confiscated includes sharpened coins, bottles, bricks, hunks of concrete, knives, bicycle spokes, plastic squirt containers filled with ammonia, stones, smoke bombs, tear-gas grenades, hammers, blackjacks, firecrackers, spiked balls, chains, and darts.[8]

The terraces are usually packed with people standing shoulder to shoulder, eating, drinking, and even urinating in place, because they are afraid to give up their positions even for a few minutes. The fans of one team are positioned at one end of the stadium cheering and jeering and yelling out insults. Separated from them by fences and lines of police, the fans of the other team stand on their terraces carrying on in the same way.

Every time a team scores a goal, their fans let out a tremendous shout, jump up and down in ecstasy, make obscene gestures, and do whatever they can to antagonize the supporters on the opposite side. The others, of course, respond in kind. The police stand between the rival fans as a kind of buffer. Whatever happens on the playing field becomes a mere backdrop to the activity in the stands. Each goal scored becomes an excuse to launch a mini-riot.

Sometimes, those attending soccer games in England seem to have an agenda that goes beyond rooting for their team. Fans have been seen wearing swastika armbands and giving Nazi salutes from the terraces. The National Front, England's neo-Nazi organization, often tries to recruit new members from among soccer fans. In the early 1980s, their magazine, *Bulldog,* retold in graphic detail the outrageous exploits of their opponents. Since 1985, police have uncovered a half-dozen gangs, including the Lunatic Fringe, the Gooners, and the thinly disguised anti-Semitic gang the Yiddos.[9]

More and more, soccer hooliganism seems to be set apart from the game itself. It is as though troubled people seize the event as an occasion to engage in random violence. This has led some experts to think of attendance at a soccer game as a kind of violent sport of and by itself. Spectators have become active participants in the game. Just standing in the terraces is a "violent experience," says one observer.[10]

Soccer in Britain seems to provide a perfect setting for outbursts of mass aggression. Opposing fans stand almost eyeball to eyeball; at the most only a few hundred yards apart. Fans share the "win at all costs" spirit and come away from the match exhausted, as though they had played themselves.

This trend toward soccer competitiveness began in the 1960s. The players played harder to win, and the fans grew more heated. According to some recent figures, the increased competitiveness has been matched with a rise in soccer injuries. The present rate is one injury for each match—about as high as for ice hockey.[11]

But what happens among the players is nothing compared to what opposing fans have done to each other. One of the most notorious incidents was the May 1985 outbreak of violence in the Heysel Stadium in Brussels. Just before the start of a final game for the European Cup, fans of the Liverpool, England, soccer club attacked the fans of their rivals, the Turin, Italy, soccer club. As the opposing groups threw bottles and bricks at each other, those below them on the terraces panicked and pushed forward. A retaining wall collapsed. Thirty-nine people were crushed to death, and 450 were badly injured.

As a result of this terrible tragedy, English professionals were banned from European competition. Twenty-six British soccer fans were arrested and forced to stand trial for their involvement in the deaths at Heysel Stadium. A six-month trial resulted in the conviction of fourteen men for involuntary manslaughter. The men were sentenced to three years in jail.

For several years English teams tried to return to European club competition. The ninety-two clubs in the four divisions of Britain's Football League appealed to the European Football Union, known by its French acronym, UEFA, to drop its ban. They improved crowd-control at home, stepped up security, installed closed-circuit television for monitoring crowd violence, introduced identity cards, and paid police to patrol the grounds. But just as the UEFA was starting to waver, English soccer fans indulged in a wild outbreak of violence at a European competition in Dusseldorf, West Germany, on June 15, 1988. Under the circumstances, England withdrew its request to have the ban lifted.

On that occasion, thousands of English fans had traveled to Dusseldorf to watch a match between England and the Netherlands. Violence broke out before, during, and after the games. For four nights, fans engaged in bouts of drunken brawling, vandalism, and street fighting. British sports minister Colin Moynihan, who was sent to Dusseldorf by Prime Minister Margaret Thatcher, said that some people had described the English troublemakers in Dusseldorf as animals. Then he added, "They [the fans] are worse than animals, because I know of no animals which would behave in this manner."[12]

Arrests of soccer fans and ejections from British stadiums have increased in recent years. In the 1986–87 season, arrests at matches in the Football League's first division rose 29 percent to 2,008, while ejections increased 45 percent to 3,532.[13] The increase in arrest numbers, however, may not mean that violence is rising, only that the problem is under tighter control.

One policeman assigned to prevent violence summed up the situation in Britain this way:

They don't even know what football is. They only know violence. I remember coming to games with my dad, and it was a joy. I mean, it was part of being a kid, you know? But I wouldn't bring my son to a game now. If he wants to see football, he has to watch it on the television. That's what these morons have done to football. They've taken it away from those of us who really love the game.[14]

Of course, soccer violence is not confined to England. One of the most infamous incidents of all time came during a three-game series between El Salvador and Honduras in June 1969. Honduras won the first game, and there was rioting in the streets by fans of both countries. El Salvador won the second game. This time, feelings ran so high that Hondurans began attacking all foreigners living in their country, causing some 10,000 Salvadorans to flee across the border. This touched off a war, but with little fighting and few casualties.[15]

At a soccer match between Peru and Argentina in May 1964, one soccer fanatic set off a riot that required police intervention with tear gas and gunfire. The fanatic, "Bomba" Rojas, a rabid Peruvian soccer fan, had a history of attacking referees. Rojas climbed a 9-foot barbed-wire fence to reach a referee whose call he didn't like. This sent the crowd stampeding to the exit gates, which were locked. Rojas survived, but 318 died in the resultant crush and 500 more were injured.[16]

To curb fan violence at soccer matches, authorities have taken some extreme measures over the years. In Moscow, a Soviet court sentenced twelve Soviet Armenian "hooligans" to terms up to twenty-five years each and confiscated their property for attempting to instigate a riot.

Perhaps most unusual, though, was the appearance of a judge dressed in robes prior to a traditional grudge match between two Bulgarian teams. An official informed all present that anyone disturbing the game would be put on trial at once. The game proceeded without incident.

RUGBY

Rugby takes its name from its birthplace, the Rugby School, in Warwickshire, England. The game suddenly began one afternoon in 1823. Willie Webb Ellis, a student, was playing in a soccer match, which followed the traditional soccer rule that prohibited use of the hands to move the ball. Frustrated because he was not able to kick the ball, Willie grabbed the ball with his hands and ran with it down the field. Some of the other players liked the idea and decided that running with the ball would make the game more fun to play and more exciting to watch. Eventually, of course, rugby football became a completely different sport from soccer.

One of the most important plays in rugby—and one of the most violent—is the scrum. A scrum is used when the ball goes out of bounds or when a ball carrier is tackled and downed and must relinquish control of the ball. In the scrum the six forwards of both teams lock arms and crouch down, head to head. The ball is then thrown through the tunnel between the two lines of the scrum, and the men in the center try to kick the ball backwards to their teammates who are standing behind them.

The scrum is responsible for some of the most serious rugby injuries. When a scrum collapses, the pressure on the front-row players can result in broken necks. An estimated twenty severe spinal injuries occur each year from rugby. In one season, five players were admitted to a Sydney, Australia, hospital either as paraplegics or quadriplegics after having scrums collapse on them.[17] Occasionally, men have been crushed and died from their rugby injuries.

As compared to American football, however, the overall rates of injury in rugby are lower and the game is generally less ferocious. From among 75,338 players in one survey, only 11,349 injuries were reported.[18] Curiously enough, the reason for the lower rate may be the lack of protective equipment. Rugby players wear only thin shirts, shorts, knee-length stockings, and cleated shoes. Without pads and other solid protective devices to use as weapons, the players have nothing that can cause some of the serious injuries caused by the helmets and other equipment of football players.

Since the 1960s, the number of rugby clubs in Britain has doubled. Television coverage has swelled, and the game has become big business. The change has put an increased pressure on clubs, coaches, and players to win. Fans no longer exhort their teams to win. Now they cry "Kill, kill, kill."

The rugby injury rate has grown by about 25 percent within the last decade according to one expert.[19] Along with the usual shoulder and knee damage, there has been a marked increase in head injuries, the result of fiercer physical contact and a rise in extracurricular violence. The rise is due, some experts say, to the greater emphasis on winning.

How can the growing violence of rugby be controlled? Participants of all ages must be coached properly and educated about the dangers of overly aggressive behavior. Coaches must stress the fundamentals of safe blocking and tackling while instilling in their players the sense that rugby is a sport played for fun, and not deadly combat.

SUMMARY

Sports violence is a serious problem in our nation. Research has provided clear proof that most competitive sports in our time increase anger and aggression in both players and viewers. Fair play is not taken seriously because more people believe, in the words of baseball manager Leo Durocher, "Nice guys finish last."

The pressure to win starts early and increases significantly by the time the athlete reaches the college and professional level of sport. For the good of the team, athletes are encouraged to play while injured, even at the risk of permanent injury. Players are often taught to regard their opponents as enemies and to play the game with hate in their hearts.

To make matters even worse, television and newspaper accounts of sporting events often emphasize particularly brutal or violent incidents. Conflicts between players and especially rough plays of vicious sports figures are featured on the nightly news.

Those who believe that sports violence is on the rise fear that viewers are becoming more and more desensitized to violence. They seek increasingly high levels of violence in sports to get the same effects. This phenomenon seems to be stronger in men, but is also found among women.

The wide promotion of sports violence must mean that few people are aware of the harmful effects. Some believe it has a cathartic effect, that it's a good way to get rid of aggression—an idea that most researchers in the field now completely reject. By becoming aware of the harmful effects of sport violence and working to improve the rules governing the various games, you can go a long way toward making competitive sports safer to play and more enjoyable to watch.

SOURCE NOTES

CHAPTER 1

1. Thomas Tutko, *Winning Is Everything and Other American Myths* (New York: Macmillan, 1976), p. 16.
2. Ibid., p. 18.
3. Ibid., p. 20.
4. Don Atyeo, *Blood and Guts: Violence in Sports* (New York: Paddington Press, 1979), p. 270.
5. Brenda Jo Bredemeier and David L. Shields, "Values and Violence in Sports Today," *Psychology Today*, October 1985, p. 23.
6. Robert C. Yeagar, *Seasons of Shame: The New Violence in Sports* (New York: McGraw-Hill, 1979), p. 10.
7. Ibid., p. 5.
8. Bredemeier, p. 25.
9. Atyeo, p. 11.
10. Jerry Kirshenbaum, "An American Disgrace," *Sports Illustrated*, 27 February 1989, p. 17.
11. Ibid., p. 18.
12. Ibid.
13. Ibid.
14. Atyeo, p. 253.
15. Ibid.

16. Robin Finn, "For Flyers Hopes Die, Not Habits," *New York Times,* 13 May 1989, p. 44.
17. Phil Galli, "Winning Is Everything," *NCTV News,* Sports Violence Issue, vol. 5, no. 1–5 (January–February 1984), p. 2.
18. Ibid.
19. Tutko, p. 4.
20. Richard M. Suinn, *Psychology in Sports: Methods and Applications* (Minneapolis: Burgess Publishing Co., 1980), p. 126.
21. Tutko, p. 41.
22. Peter Alfano, "On the Black Market, Drugs Are in Easy Reach of Public: Steroids in Sports," *New York Times,* 18 November 1988, pp. A1, A22.
23. Tutko, p. 16.
24. Atyeo, p. 246.
25. Charles Leerhsen, "When Push Comes to Shove," *Newsweek,* 16, May 1988, p. 72.
26. Ibid.
27. James F. Clarity, "Longer Seasons and Shorter Fuses," *New York Times,* 15 May 1988, sec. 4, p. 9.
28. Tutko, p. 4.
29. Ibid., p. 15.

CHAPTER 2

1. Robert C. Yeagar, *Seasons of Shame: The New Violence in Sports* (New York: McGraw-Hill, 1979), pp. 19, 20.
2. Bruce Nash and Allan Zullo, *The Sports Hall of Shame* (New York: Pocket Books, 1987), p. 143.
3. Robert Daley, *The Cruel Sport* (New York: Bonanza, 1958), unpaged.
4. Frederick C. Klein, "On Sports: Death in the 'Brickyard,' " *Wall Street Journal,* 27 May 1988, p. 15.
5. Daley.
6. Don Atyeo, *Blood and Guts: Violence in Sports* (New York: Paddington Press, 1979), p. 340.
7. Klein, p. 15.
8. Atyeo, p. 344.
9. Ibid., p. 340.
10. Ibid., p. 341.
11. Daley.
12. Atyeo, p. 349.
13. Daley.
14. Ibid.

15. Ibid.
16. Stewart McBride, "Racing's Record-Breaker," *New York Times Magazine*, 8 November 1987, p. 44.
17. Ibid.
18. Nash, p. 133.
19. Daley.
20. Klein, p. 15.
21. "Petty Raps 'Safety Rules,' " *Newsday*, 18 February 1988, p. 135.

CHAPTER 3

1. Marty Noble, "Mets' Lightning Can't Strike Twice," *New York Times*, 2 June 1988, p. 16.
2. R. Brasch, *How Did Sports Begin?* (New York: David McKay, Inc.), 1970, p. 38.
3. Hank Hersch, "It's War Out There," *Sports Illustrated*, 20 July 1987, p. 17.
4. Ibid.
5. Don Atyeo, *Blood and Guts: Violence in Sports* (New York: Paddington Press, 1979), p. 270.
6. Hersch, p. 14.
7. Ibid.
8. Robert C. Yeagar, *Seasons of Shame: The New Violence in Sports* (New York: McGraw-Hill, 1979), p. 154.
9. Atyeo, p. 268.
10. Ibid.
11. Charles Leerhsen, "When Push Comes to Shove," *Newsweek*, 16 May 1988, p. 72.
12. Ibid.
13. Tim Braine and John Stravinsky, *The Not-So-Great Moments in Sports* (New York: Morrow, 1986), p. 237.
14. Atyeo, p. 269.
15. Ibid.
16. Braine, p. 160.
17. Yaegar, p. 80.
18. Craig Neff, "Can It Happen in the U.S.?" *Sports Illustrated*, 10 June 1985, p. 27.
19. Peter Gammons, "Inside Baseball: Mayhem By the Bay," *Sports Illustrated*, 8 August 1988, p. 64.
20. William Oscar Johnson, "Sports and Suds," *Sports Illustrated*, 8 August 1988, p. 70.
21. Ibid., p. 80.
22. Ibid., p. 78.

23. Ibid., pp. 77–78.
24. Ibid., p. 80.

CHAPTER 4

1. Don Atyeo, *Blood and Guts: Violence in Sports* (New York: Paddington Press, 1979), p. 271.
2. Ibid.
3. William C. Rhoden, "Big East Studies Curbs on Fighting," *New York Times*, 23 February 1988, pp. A25, A28.
4. Atyeo, p. 271.
5. Rhoden, p. A25.
6. R. Brasch, *How Did Sports Begin?* (New York: David McKay Co., 1970), p. 42.
7. Peter Alfano, "Battling Athletes Hurt Sports' Image," *New York Times*, 8 February 1988, pp. C2, C4.
8. Atyeo, p. 272.
9. Bruce Nash and Allan Zullo, *The Sports Hall of Shame* (New York: Pocket Books, 1987), p. 9.
10. Ibid., p. 14.
11. Robert C. Yeagar, *Seasons of Shame: The New Violence in Sports* (New York: McGraw-Hill, 1979), pp. C1, C4.
12. Nash, p. 20.
13. Atyeo, p. 273.
14. Ibid., p. 272.
15. Craig Neff, "Can It Happen in the U.S.?" *Sports Illustrated*, 10 June 1985, p. 27.
16. Ibid.
17. "Violence Jeopardizes Tourney," *Newsday*, 19 January 1988, p. 21.
18. Dan Fagin, "Shots Fired in Basketball Rivalry," *Newsday*, 29 February 1988, p. 7.

CHAPTER 5

1. George D. Lundberg, "Boxing Should Be Banned in Civilized Countries," editorial, *Journal of the American Medical Association*, 9 May 1986, vol. 255, no. 18, p. 2483.
2. Ibid.
3. Jeffrey T. Sammons, "Let's Knock Prizefighting Out of the Ring," *Newsday*, 24 June 1988, p. 93.
4. Thomas Radecki, "Boxing Protested at Pan-American Games," press release, International Coalition Against Violent Entertainment, 14 August 1987.

5. Don Atyeo, *Blood and Guts: Violence in Sports* (New York: Paddington Press, 1979), p. 22.
6. John V. Gromback, *The Saga of the Fist* (South Brunswick, N.J.: A. S. Barnes, 1977), p. 22.
7. Joyce Carol Oates, *On Boxing* (New York: Doubleday, 1987), p. 41.
8. Atyeo, p. 178.
9. Oates, p. 48.
10. Sammons, p. 93.
11. R. G. Morrison, "Boxing," *Journal of the American Medical Association*, 9 May 1986, vol. 255, no. 18, p. 2476.
12. Atyeo, p. 156.
13. Oates, p. 98.
14. Ibid.
15. Ibid., p. 10.
16. Radecki.
17. Ibid.
18. Atyeo, p. 169.
19. Ibid., p. 176.
20. Ibid.
21. Radecki.
22. Jeffrey T. Sammons, *Beyond the Ring* (Urbana: University of Illinois Press, 1988), p. 229.
23. Bruce Nash and Allan Zullo, *The Sports Hall of Shame* (New York: Pocket Books, 1987), p. 192.
24. Atyeo, p. 180.
25. Keay Davidson, "Study Links Boxing, Homicide," *Newsday*, 11 August 1983, p. 13.
26. Lundberg, p. 2484.
27. Oates, p. 93.
28. Sammons, *Beyond the Ring*, p. 252.
29. Atyeo, p. 163–64.
30. Ralph Schoenstein, "Dark Tales From Ringside," *50-Plus*, May 1985, v. 25, p. 27.

CHAPTER 6

1. Robert Sullivan, "Scorecard," *Sports Illustrated*, 15 December 1986, v. 65, p. 17.
2. Ibid.
3. Rich Cimini, "Williams: When I Hit, I Hurt You," *Newsday*, 21 May 1988, p. 33.
4. Rich Cimini, "What, Us Dirty? Oilers' Glenville Calls It Bad Rap," *Newsday*, 15 September 1988, p. 35.

5. Rick Kellogg, "Defensive 'Missile' Guides Seahawks," *New York Times,* 9 November 1987, p. 28.
6. Don Atyeo, *Blood and Guts: Violence in Sports* (New York: Paddington Press, 1979), p. 192.
7. R. Brasch, *How Did Sports Begin?* (New York: David McKay, Inc., 1970), p. 149.
8. Atyeo, p. 200.
9. Ibid., p. 208.
10. "Sports Injuries," *Accident Facts: 1988 Edition,* National Safety Council, p. 83.
11. Kellogg, p. 28.
12. Atyeo, p. 221.
13. Ibid.
14. Vincent M. Mallozzi, "More Is Less," *New York Times,* 13 February 1989, p. C2.
15. "The Buoniconti Tackle Paralysis," *Sports Illustrated,* 15 December 1986, v. 65, p. 17.
16. Atyeo, p. 223.
17. Robert C. Yeagar, *Seasons of Shame: The New Violence in Sports* (New York: McGraw-Hill, 1979), p. 15.
18. "Bronco Is Fined," *New York Times,* 25 September 1988, sec. 8, p. 14.
19. Rich Cimini, "Jets Win by Knockout," *Newsday,* 19 September 1988, pp. 97, 112.
20. Atyeo, p. 247.
21. Ibid., p. 248.
22. Ibid., p. 251.
23. Ibid.
24. Ibid. p. 253.
25. Frank Litsky, "Giants' Taylor, In New Book Says He Used Cocaine Often," *New York Times,* 24 July 1987, pp. A1, B16.
26. Atyeo, p. 370.
27. Melvin Berger, *Sports Medicine* (New York: Crowell, 1982), p. 50.
28. Ibid., p. 58.

CHAPTER 7

1. Bruce Nash and Allan Zullo, *The Sports Hall of Shame* (New York: Pocket Books, 1987), p. 64.
2. Jim Smith, "Isles Put Bodies on Line," *Newsday,* 18 February 1988, p. 152.
3. "Flyers' Brown Suspended for 15 Games," *New York Times,* 3 November 1987, pp. A25, A27.

4. Robin Finn, "Winning and Not Revenge Is Propp's Goal for Flyers, *New York Times*, 3 May 1989, p. B10.
5. Joe Sexton, "O'Neill Answers Calls of Violence," *New York Times*, 21 November 1988, pp. C1, C6.
6. "Ranger Injury Report," *New York Times*, 11 November 1987, p. B14.
7. Don Atyeo, *Blood and Guts: Violence in Sports* (New York: Paddington Press, 1979), p. 230.
8. Ibid., p. 231.
9. E. M. Swift, "The NHL Isn't So Tough; If It Were, It Would Crack Down on Gratuitous Violence," column, *Sports Illustrated*, 12 October 1987, v. 64, p. 122.
10. National Safety Council, *Accident Facts, 1988 Edition*, p. 83.
11. Nash, p. 56.
12. Atyeo, p. 257.
13. Nash, p. 47.
14. Atyeo, p. 258.
15. Ibid.
16. Ibid., p. 262.
17. Thomas Tutko, *Winning Is Everything and Other American Myths* (New York: Macmillan, 1976), p. 17.
18. Sexton, p. C6.
19. Ibid.
20. Tim Braine and John Stravinsky, *The Not-So-Great Moments in Sports* (New York: William Morrow, 1986), p. 236.
21. "Question of the Week: 'Can the N.H.L. Stop Sticking Incidents?' " *New York Times*, 3 November 1988, sec. 8., p. 11.
22. Ibid.

CHAPTER 8

1. Don Atyeo, *Blood and Guts: Violence in Sports* (New York: Paddington Press, 1979), p. 348.
2. Bruce Nash and Allan Zullo, *The Sports Hall of Shame* (New York: Pocket Books, 1987), p. 126.
3. Steven Crist, "In Winner's Circle, Jockey Is Mourned," *New York Times*, 15 October 1988, p. 58.
4. Atyeo, p. 342.
5. Ibid.
6. Ibid., p. 348.
7. Ibid., p. 351.
8. Robert Yeagar, *Seasons of Shame* (New York: McGraw-Hill, 1979), p. 34.

9. Crist, p. 58.
10. Tim Braine and John Stravinsky, *The Not-So-Great Moments in Sports* (New York: Morrow, 1986), p. 38.

CHAPTER 9

1. Steve Lohr, "93 Die in Crush at British Soccer Game," *New York Times,* 16 April 1989, p. 12.
2. Robert Thomas, Jr., "English Fall to Soviets," *New York Times,* 19 June 1988, sec 8., p. 1.
3. Lesley Hazleton, "British Soccer: The Deadly Game," *New York Times Magazine,* p. 40.
4. Lohr, p. 12.
5. Ibid.
6. R. Brasch, *How Did Sports Begin?* (New York: David McKay Co., 1970), p. 151.
7. Steve Lohr, "Soccer Alert: The British (Fans) Are Coming!" *New York Times,* 10 June 1988, p. D22.
8. Hazleton, p. 40.
9. Ibid.
10. Craig R. Whitney, "The Rage That Is Unleashed in the Soccer Stadiums," *New York Times,* 23 April 1989, p. E3.
11. Hazleton, p. 40.
12. "Soccer City Arms Itself for Rioters," *Newsday,* 16 June 1988, p. 176.
13. Lohr, "Soccer Alert," p. D22.
14. Hazleton, p. 40.
15. Bruce Nash and Allan Zullo, *The Sports Hall of Shame,* (New York: Pocket Books, 1987), p. 227.
16. Ibid.
17. Don Atyeo, *Blood and Guts: Violence in Sports* (New York: Paddington Press, 1979), p. 284.
18. Ibid., p. 290.
19. Ibid.

BIBLIOGRAPHY

NEWSPAPERS AND MAGAZINES

New York Times
"British Soccer: The Deadly Game," 7 May 1987.
"More Is Less," 13 February 1989.
"O'Neill Answers Call of Violence," 21 November 1988.

Newsweek
"When Push Comes to Shove," 16 May 1988.

Psychology Today
"Values and Violence in Sports Today," October 1985.

Sports Illustrated
"Can It Happen in the U.S.?" 10 June 1985.
"Sports and Suds," 8 August 1988.
"An American Disgrace," 27 February 1989.

PUBLICATIONS

Journal of the American Medical Association
"Brain Injury in Boxing," 1983.

Congressional Record
"Sports Violence Arbitration Act: Proceedings and Debates of the 99th Congress," 20 November 1985.

BOOKS

Atyeo, Don. *Blood and Guts: Violence in Sports.* New York: Paddington Press, 1979.

Goldstein, J. H. *Sports Violence.* New York: Springer-Verlag, 1983.

Smith, Michael. *Violence and Sport.* Toronto: Butterworths, 1983.

Yeagar, Robert C. *Seasons of Shame: The New Violence in Sports.* New York: McGraw-Hill, 1979.

INDEX